Far Away from the Tigers

*

Far Away from the Tigers

*

A Year in the Classroom with Internationally Adopted Children

*

Jane Katch

*

THE UNIVERSITY OF CHICAGO PRESS

CHICAGO AND LONDON

Jane Katch

has been teaching and writing about young children
for over thirty years; after *Under Deadman's Skin:
Discovering the Meaning of Children's Violent Play* and
*They Don't Like Me: Lessons on Bullying and Teasing
from a Preschool Classroom*, this is her third book. She
currently teaches kindergarten at the Touchstone
Community School in Grafton, Massachusetts.

The University of Chicago Press, Chicago 60637
The University of Chicago Press, Ltd., London
© 2011 by Jane Katch
All rights reserved. Published 2011
Printed in the United States of America

20 19 18 17 16 15 14 13 12 11   1 2 3 4 5

Little Peep drawings courtesy of Caleb.

ISBN-13: 978-0-226-42578-8 (cloth)
ISBN-10: 0-226-42578-9 (cloth)

Library of Congress Cataloging-in-Publication Data
Katch, Jane.
Far away from the tigers : a year in the classroom with
internationally adopted children / Jane Katch.
p. cm.
ISBN-13: 978-0-226-42578-8 (cloth : alk. paper)
ISBN-10: 0-226-42578-9 (cloth : alk. paper) 1. Adopted
children—Education—United States. 2. Adopted
children—Education—United States—
Psychological aspects. 3. Early childhood
education—United States. I. Title.
LC3723.K38 2011
372.182'54—dc22
2010032583

♾ The paper used in this publication meets the minimum
requirements of the American National Standard for
Information Sciences—Permanence of Paper for Printed
Library Materials, ANSI Z39.48–1992.

For Vivian

Oh wailing messenger,
Oh baleful, full-bodied crier
of the abandoned and the chosen,
Oh trumpet of laughter, oh Gabriel,
joy everlasting . . .

FROM "THE WELCOMING" BY EDWARD HIRSCH

Contents

Acknowledgments

I would like to give my deepest thanks to the people who have done so much to make this book possible:

* to Jed for everything.
* to Margaret and Hannah for their help, encouragement, and love.
* to the three families who have taught me so much about international adoption.
* to Touchstone Community School for encouraging and supporting my work.
* to Elizabeth Branch Dyson for understanding what was most important and for supporting me in so many ways, to Anne Summers Goldberg for her cheerful help with all the details, and to Ruth Goring for her thoughtful editing.
* to the Still River writers, again.

Questions

"I'm reluctant to say this," Gwen says to me. "This is going to make you feel terrible." The air in Robert and Lynn's living room becomes electric as we all wait for her to tell me something awful.

I have asked Gwen, Robert, and Lynn to talk with me about some of the concerns they had when they first brought their internationally adopted children to school. These children have been in my kindergarten class for four months, and although I have unanswered questions about them, I am confident they are having a good year. Still, while Gwen takes a breath and prepares to continue, I have time to be aware of a tightening in my stomach.

She begins. "When we came for our first conference with you, I told you about Jasper's[1] adoption from Cambodia. He was obviously adopted—look at me!" Gwen pushes a few wisps of curly red hair away from her face, toward her ponytail. "After the conference I saw Robert, who had already finished his conference with you about Katya, and I said, 'I don't know about this class; I don't know about this teacher. I don't think she likes adopted kids.'"

We laugh nervously. Lynn, Katya's mother, tries to smooth over the tension. "Because you misread it—too bad," she says to Gwen. I appreciate Lynn's assumption that Gwen had simply misunderstood, but did I have a part in this misunderstanding? I am startled by Gwen's criticism: I like to think I listen carefully to parents and

---

1. The names of students in this book have been changed, as have identifying details, to protect the privacy of the individuals involved. In addition, some of the characters are based on composites of more than one child.

respect them. At the same time I recognize the value of her over-coming her reluctance to be honest with me. And I am curious.

"Do you remember what I did that gave you that feeling?" I ask.

"As we were talking," she tells me, "I said something about an area where Jasper was behind developmentally; maybe just that he's not social or that he talks less than other kids. And you said, 'Well, we don't know what he was exposed to before you brought him home. There's all kinds of things that could have gone wrong in his cognitive development back then.' And the way I heard it was, 'Well, you've got a defective kid, so we'll do the best we can with him.' And I walked out of there thinking, 'She's already labeled my child as a failure because he was defective before I picked him up.' I wanted to run back in and say, 'He was six months old when we adopted him,' and tell you my whole story and bring in the pictures and get defensive and say, 'This is not the issue. This is him; this is not his adoption.' And I think part of it—when I walked out of your classroom that day—I wished I could have avoided telling you about his adoption. I wished that it wasn't obvious, because it's painful. I wished we could have just let it go and said nothing."

In my mind I replay that fall conference day. In the morning Caleb's mother, Golda, had told me that a pediatrician specializing in international adoptions said that Caleb has language difficulties resulting from his deprived infancy in Romania. Later that morning Robert and Lynn had told me that they believed Katya's difficulties around food and relationships went back to her early deprivation in a Russian orphanage. In the afternoon of that same conference day, knowing nothing about Cambodia or about Jasper's early life, I had assumed his avoidance of playing with other children might go back to his infancy in Cambodia: I had prejudged him before having any specific information. I recount the sequence to Gwen and say that I think she has a good point.

"I misread it and I was defensive, and I'm sure that was me bring-ing things to the table also," Gwen says. "Anxiety about a new en-vironment, new teacher, how you'd respond to my kid—the same thing all parents have in a new situation. But what I walk away with is that I think adoptive parents enter every new situation on the defensive."

For the last five years my previously white, middle-class kindergarten has included increasing numbers of children from international adoptions. Their faces, most often shades of brown, give my class a diverse look that I welcome: since leaving a lab school at an urban university, I have missed the wider variety of young faces and the assortment of world languages in my room.

Still, I have begun to realize that there is much I do not know about teaching these children. Caleb, a six-year-old from Romania, is the oldest child in the class. His language is hard to follow: he jumbles thoughts and sentences, leaving out important information and linking diverse fragments that don't seem connected. I believe he needs to learn to speak coherently before he can learn to read, but how will I help him get ready for first grade? Jasper, from Cambodia, sits silently at a table practicing the alphabet in uppercase, lowercase, and cursive, while the other boys in the room build a puppy pound in the block area nearby. Should he be encouraged to join them, or should I let him be alone? Katya, adopted from Russia, wants everyone's attention all the time. She disrupts morning meeting and keeps the girls' social group in an uproar. But if her first years in a Russian orphanage were harsh, how can I deal with her manipulative behavior without adding to her trauma?

There's a second set of questions too: What is the best way for me to approach their parents? Do they want to talk with me about their adoptions? Are there questions I should either ask or avoid?

I start looking for answers. On the Internet, I learn that my class is not the only place seeing a dramatic rise in the numbers of internationally adopted children. In 1994, eight thousand Americans adopted children from abroad. Between 2001 and 2007, there were around twenty thousand international adoptions each year. Increasingly I'm seeing little Chinese girls in Asian restaurants with their adoptive parents.

I look for books on the subject. I find books full of information about developing a healthy relationship with adopted children, and I find resources for understanding medical and developmental problems that might arise, but these do not help me figure out what to do with my three puzzling children. I arrange for a social worker specializing in adoption to come to a faculty meeting to tell us what we should know. She focuses on helping teachers avoid embarrassing adopted students: don't ask them to bring in baby pictures, don't do a unit on the family tree that implies that all children know their biological roots, don't talk about "real mothers" and "real fathers." This is useful information, but when I ask her how I can handle Katya's manipulation without causing her to feel rejected by me, she does not know.

Not discovering answers from the "experts," I decide to go to those who know the children best: I invite the parents of all three children to have a series of conversations with me about their experiences starting their children in school. Caleb's mother, Golda, is not able to join us for the first gathering but will talk with me another day.

So I find myself now on a comfortable couch at Katya's house, talking with her parents, Lynn and Robert, and with Jasper's mother, Gwen, about their experiences bringing their children to daycare and eventually into my kindergarten: how much did they want to tell teachers and child care workers about their adoption experiences, and what kinds of conversations were most useful?

Listening to the parents and observing the children, I begin to find answers to some of my questions. In the process, I find that the questions need to change: my original wish to "fix" the children's problems turns into a growing respect for the inner strength of the parents and the children.

Part One

*

The Lucky Ones

1

Happily Ever After

"One little puppy, sitting on a log. One fell off and bumped his head.
And then he saw a fire engine. And then he lived happily ever after."

Caleb and I are sitting at a small round table in my kindergarten
class. We call it the story table, because it is where I sit each morning to write down the stories that the children dictate to me. Later
in the day we will act these stories out, and Caleb will get to choose
which character he wants to play.

Caleb's story puzzles me. I stop writing and look at him. He tears
a long piece of masking tape from the dispenser and wraps it several times around empty toilet-paper rolls that he is attaching to
the bottom of a cardboard box formerly containing unsalted butter.
"This is the fire engine," he says, attaching a Popsicle stick that may
represent the hose or ladder.

Caleb is the oldest child in the class. I've been puzzled about him
since I first saw him standing just inside the classroom door on the
day of our kindergarten screening. Seven other children built with
blocks, dressed up, listened to a story, and ate snacks while Caleb
stood at the entrance, his shoulders hunched, hands in his pockets,
black curls almost hiding his dark eyes.

His language, too, was unusual: his mumbled refusals to our suggestions that he come in and join the play did not contain the letter
substitutions often made by young children, but were a jumble of
phrases that seemed random and were hard to follow.

An hour later, the story table was covered with applications and
school records, and I sat with the three other teachers who had
observed the group. We learned that Caleb had been adopted from
Romania when he was almost three. At that time, he spoke only a

few words and was suffering from malnutrition and severe developmental delays.

Golda had told our admissions director that Caleb's pediatrician, a specialist in internationally adopted children, said Caleb needed a small language-based classroom in addition to his ongoing speech therapy. The local public school had thirty-two children, and Golda knew it was the wrong place for him.

Remembering the news stories and videotapes of starving Romanian orphans, we all wanted to give Caleb a chance: might he just need more time to learn English? Although he was chronologically old enough for first grade, we could give him an extra year of kindergarten. Could the small and inclusive community at our independent school help him feel secure enough to give up his worried stance at the door and come in?

Now, a half-year later, as I am wondering why the puppy fell off the log and what the fire engine was doing in the woods, I'm still not sure if I am giving Caleb what he needs. In conversation, he leaves out information that is necessary for his listeners to understand him. Many of his stories change plot or characters midstream. He loves to use big words, but either his pronunciation or his meaning is often a bit off.

He has been learning to play with other children, listening to what they want in a game and incorporating their ideas into his plans. I am hoping that a curriculum emphasizing stories and conversation will help him to speak more coherently before he has to tackle the more abstract tasks of reading and writing.

I decide not to ask him about the puppy and the fire engine. Many children enjoy such conversations, using the opportunity to expand their ideas. Caleb, on the other hand, tends to experience questions about his stories as criticism rather than useful clarification. But once the roles are given out and the children are trying to follow his directions, he will want to describe the action as clearly as he can so the story comes to life in the way he imagined.

Vivian Paley, who invented this activity, calls it "doing stories."[1]

1. Vivian Paley, *Wally's Stories* (Cambridge, MA: Harvard University Press, 1981).

The storytellers expand their abilities to tell coherent and interesting plots while the actors must listen carefully so they know what to do next. In the process, they all come to share and respect each other's fantasies, creating a close community through language.

"So when we act this out we'll need a puppy," I say to Caleb. "Do you want someone to be the fire engine?"

"I'm the puppy," he says. "And there's five firemen, 'cause they're the rescuers."

"How do they rescue you?" I ask, forgetting, in my surprise, my resolve to wait and see.

"'Cause I was in a fire," he says.

When Caleb finishes telling his story he moves into the block area. "Who wants to be an FBI guy with me?" he asks Shawn and Glen, who have already started taking large, hollow wooden blocks off the shelf.

The other boys have no difficulty with his language skills, and they are immediately interested in his ideas. "Good! We got our steering wheels!" Caleb says, making a stack of blocks, sitting on them, one leg on each side, and putting a semicircular block in front of him.

"This is my place," Shawn says, building an exact replica next to him. There is an excitement in Caleb's ideas that frequently makes him a leader in play.

"Motorcycles coming up!" Caleb announces. The boys make the sound of roaring engines, just below the decibel level at which I would have demanded more quiet.

"The stock pipes!" Caleb says, picking up a long block and setting it down at the rear of his motorcycle.

"Stock pipes?" I ask from the table nearby where I have been eavesdropping.

"The smoke comes out," he explains.

Ah, exhaust pipes.

"Boston! Where is Boston?" Glen, now on a third motorcycle, asks.

"Are you going to Boston? 'Cause I can, too!" Caleb says.

"I'm going to find the bad guys," Glen announces. "I went through the tunnel and there's a bad guy in the city. I'm gonna fire!"

"Glen," Caleb says, "I gotta go to the police station!"

Caleb's plots almost always end up in the police station. Caleb's police are protectors, keeping his protagonists safe from robbers and defending puppies from bad guys who would take them to the pound. His adoptive mother thinks he may have a very early memory of the police coming at night to take him from his neglectful family.

Could his fascination with police be the result of this early trauma? There is so much about him that I do not know.

In play, communication can be made up of disconnected shouted headlines: "Where is Boston?" follows the demand for exhaust pipes and is interrupted by the entrance of the bad guys. Caleb's tendency to leave out important connections is not a problem in the block area.

But telling a coherent story requires more complex language skills. When we gather around the rug, our stage, an hour later to act out the morning's stories, Caleb must fill in the gaps in his story so everyone can understand it.

I give out the parts. Caleb is the puppy and five volunteers are the firemen. Then I read the story Caleb has dictated, pausing after each phrase while the actors perform the actions:

"One little puppy, sitting on a log. One fell off and bumped his head."

Caleb comes into the middle of the rug, sits down, and falls over, rubbing his head.

"And then he saw a fire engine. And then he lived happily ever after."

Katya, one of the five firefighters arriving on the scene, looks puzzled. "Is there a fire?" she asks Caleb.

"Here!" Caleb says, pointing to the invisible log beside him. Katya ad-libs the missing part: "There's the fire! Over there! Bring the hoses!" The firefighters excitedly spray invisible water all around.

Glen, one of the firemen, reaches out a hand to help Caleb up.

Unlike my questions, which confuse Caleb, the actors show him what critical information we need in order to proceed.

"Now *that's* happily ever after," Katya tells Caleb.

* 2 *

A Long Road

I did not want to hear about Caleb's orphanage in Romania. I remembered the images in the media in 1989 when the dictator, Nicolae Ceaușescu, was overthrown and the orphanages were opened: malnourished children, neglected in their cribs, many at two and three years old unable to walk or talk. Under the dictatorship, laws had required women to have four or five children before being able to obtain birth control or an abortion. Many parents, too poor to support such a large family, had taken some of their children to orphanages. Eighty percent of them were Roma, who were viewed as undesirable.

But if Caleb had had to live through such difficult infant and toddler years, the least I could do was be willing to learn about them. So I arranged to meet Caleb's mother, Golda, at the business she owns and runs in a nearby city. The demands of her work make it hard for her to take time away; she had not been able to meet with the other parents at Robert and Lynn's house, but she offered to meet me at lunchtime to tell me about her trip to Bucharest to get Caleb.

We sit down in a quiet section of her office. "First I thought I would adopt from Russia," she explains. "I went to a meeting with a woman from an adoption agency. I said to her, 'I am not interested in a special needs kid. I can't do it. It's not in my nature.'

"That woman talked like a social worker: 'You have every right, every right, to want a child that's normal,'" Golda mimics an overly sweet tone.

"Well, here I am. I switched to Romania because Russia was going to close down for international adoption for some reason. They're always opening and closing countries. So I looked at the

Romanian kids and they looked like me, I guess. I'm Italian but I became Jewish and changed my name to Golda," she explains, "and the Gypsy kids, they call them Roma now, looked like someone from my Italian family. So I just switched to Romania. And I was gonna get a girl, because of course I don't have any male role models, since I'm a single mother, but a guy I work with had two adopted kids and he said, 'I think it would be so helpful for you to raise a son,' maybe because I already have raised a daughter. She's in college now. And I drove back, went to TJ Maxx, looked at the clothes, and said, 'OK, I can do this.' Because I had bought tons of girls' clothes, because I'm a shopper. And then I started buying boys' clothes.

"And they sent me a video of a child. And my sister, who's a social worker, said to me, 'These kids have big problems—these kids have big problems.' But at that point you're so vulnerable; you're just vulnerable. So I would listen, but they never mentioned early intervention. They never mentioned anything like that. All they said was, 'They catch up.' And I'm like, 'OK, they catch up.'"

A ten-year study of children adopted in Canada from Romanian orphanages in 1990–91 showed that at the time of adoption virtually all had medical and developmental problems. In general, the longer the Romanian children had lived in the orphanage the more problems they had, and the longer they lived in Canada the fewer they had. After three years, more than one-third of the Romanian orphans had recovered fully from the neglect they experienced in early childhood, one-third had a few serious problems but were progressing toward average levels of performance and behavior, but almost a third of those who had been adopted after eight months of age still had several serious problems.[1] Ten years after adoption, many of them continued to have difficulties with attention and self-regulation.[2]

1. Elinor W. Ames et al., *The Development of Romanian Orphanage Children Adopted to Canada: Final Report, Romanian Adoption Project* (Burnaby, BC: Simon Fraser University, 1997).

2. Karyn Audet, "Attentional and Self-Regulatory Difficulties of Romanian Orphans Ten Years after Being Adopted to Canada: A Longitudinal Study" (Burnaby, BC: Simon Fraser University, 2003), available at ir.lib.sfu.ca/bitstream /1892/9837/1/b31550022.pdf (accessed July 10, 2010).

Although recently the general health and development of newly arrived Romanian adoptees is said to have improved,[3] in 1997, a year before Golda was considering adoption from Romania, Elinor Ames published a study for the Canadian government, recommending that all Romanian adoptions be considered by both prospective parents and adoption officials to be special needs adoptions. She wrote, "Like other special-needs adoptions, e.g., those of physically or mentally handicapped children, adoption of orphanage children must be acknowledged to involve extra commitments of parents' time, energy, acquisition of expertise, and willingness to work with helping agencies."[4]

I do not imagine that Golda was aware of the report at the time, but I wonder if social workers at the adoption agency had seen it.

"So they sent me a video of a little boy," Golda continues. "He was probably four at the time. And we looked at the video—my sister, my mother, everybody looked at it. And he was cute. He was Roma, too. But he didn't spark my interest. He didn't look like the kind of kid that was gonna do the kind of things I want to do."

"What did you hope he would do?" I ask.

"Get up at three in the morning to go to the Vineyard, like my crazy lifestyle, and be creative.

"And then we saw this," she continues, while she puts a video in the VCR that's sitting on her desk. I see a toddler with Caleb's dark eyes and thick black hair, pushing a little car back and forth with a caregiver. She smiles and talks animatedly with him, trying to get him to smile back at her. When she succeeds, it's Caleb at his most irresistible, his whole face animated and joyful.

"And we said, 'Look at that! He's left-handed! That means he's creative!' And my mother and sister said, 'Oh, my god, look at that kid! That is your kid!' He was just as defiant and ornery!"

"I can see why you fell in love with him when you saw this," I say.

3. Laurie C. Miller, *The Handbook of International Adoption Medicine* (New York: Oxford University Press, 2005), 58.

4. Elinor W. Ames, *Recommendations from the Final Report: The Development of Romanian Orphanage Children Adopted to Canada*, study funded by National Welfare Grants Program, Human Resources Development, Government of Canada, 1997.

"And I think that's what saved him. You know, my mother is always saying he's not like any of us: he's a real extrovert, one of those people who will go up to you and just draw you in. That's something that he was born with.

"This was November and he was two." Caleb rolls a big soft ball to the caregiver. "They bulked him up with clothes to make him look fat," Golda says. "When I got him, he weighed twenty-four and a half pounds and he was two and a half. He was at the bottom of the chart for his age."

"What about his head circumference?" I ask, remembering from my reading that having short stature and being underweight are not as worrisome as having a small head circumference.[5] In children from orphanages, a small head usually reflects early brain injury. It may reduce IQ and increase the likelihood of a wide range of problems that can involve learning disabilities, poor academic performance, problematic behavior, and diminished executive functioning.

"The doctor here said it wasn't bad. She had me feed him a lot of fats the first year, to get it back. He improved and the doctor kept saying, 'My colleagues would be amazed at this head circumference recovery because they say it's not recoverable.'"

We watch Caleb, as a toddler, climbing a flight of stairs while holding on to the railing. "He's two and he's holding on," she says. "He should be walking by himself."

Caleb toddles over to a small tricycle, climbs on, and falls off. "He does OK," Golda says, "but his muscle tone is a little off."

What strikes me, though, is how active and curious Caleb appears in this video, in contrast to Ames's descriptions of Romanian orphanages in the early 1990s, when she found most babies and nontoddling "toddlers" uninterested and unresponsive.[6]

"He was the pet of the orphanage—we know that because of

5. Miller, *Handbook of International Adoption Medicine*, 186.
6. Elinor W. Ames, "Orphanage Experiences Play a Key Role in Adopted Romanian Children's Development," http://www.nacac.org/adoptalk/orphanageexperiences.html (accessed July 10, 2010).

the way they were kissing and hugging him. They did a lot of stuff with him in this video, so to me that means they had an investment in him being given an opportunity. They said the woman who took care of him couldn't come the day he was leaving because she was too upset. So he got the most food, I'm sure. Potatoes and pasta, they gave him. The minute he got out to Bucharest, he ate ham and spinach, and he just ate and ate and ate."

His caregiver picks him up and tickles his cheek. Golda explains that it is uncommon in these videos for a caregiver to hold a child and that it's also unusual that he was wearing shoes.

"That's a big thing," Golda says. "If you have shoes it means you're a pet."

We watch Caleb's caregiver play some keys on a piano and he copies her, laughing. His nose is running. Golda explains that there were fifty children in the orphanage with about four or five care-givers. The orphanage had just been renovated and was very clean. "But he was sick in this video; he had a cold. When we picked him up, he was still sick. They didn't buy him the medicine because we were coming for him. It cost fourteen cents."

We watch Caleb standing by a baby that is lying on its back under a hanging mobile, and Golda explains that it was his job to watch them. He was in charge of the babies because he was the oldest. According to the rules he should have been moved to the larger orphanage at age two, but since he was waiting for her, he was able to stay an extra six months. The adoption agency people were fight-ing with their contact in Romania—they said she had stolen some money that was supposed to be going to a relief program. "And for months I kept getting this runaround," Golda says, "so finally I just said, 'You better tell them I'm coming, because I'm coming and it's a done deal.' So I just went, not knowing if I could get him. I wasn't going to wait any more. By rights I shouldn't have waited six months; I should have waited maybe a month. Now Romania is closed for international adoption except for grandparents. They're trying to put kids in foster homes. They say in Romania they were selling them on the black market. There was a whole controversy."

When Golda was in Budapest, she had heard that Caleb's mother was in the next village, but she was not allowed to go there. It was a Roma family, and Caleb's mother was sixteen. "She was a kid!" Golda tells me. "She was living with her mother and her grandmother and her four or five siblings in two rooms. They didn't know who the father was—it was from a casual relationship. There was heat in just one room, and Caleb was severely malnourished. They took him from her for neglect."

He was breastfed, probably because the family was very poor. It's not clear what age he was when he was taken from his mother; it may have been two or three months, Golda says. His mother would return to the hospital to breastfeed him, and then she was supposed to come get him by a certain time. She didn't do it, so he was placed in the orphanage at about nine months. In August of that year, before he turned two, she relinquished her rights, and he was put up for adoption. "In October they started looking for adoptive parents, Golda says. "I got the video in November, when he turned two.

"I've been searching for his mother for almost five years now, in different ways. I searched over the Internet, I sent letters to everyone with her name, I even put a dollar in each one to write back, but nobody sent them back. Now I've found someone who's been doing these searches in Romania for years, so we'll see what happens."

"What was it like when you brought him home?" I ask.

"He was fine on the plane," she says. "They gave him phenobarbital. I didn't know why he was falling asleep. The taxi driver that took us to Bucharest said, 'They gave him some drugs.'"

I think about the irony that he was not given the medication he needed when he was sick but he was medicated without notification of his new mother when he left. I give the caregivers the benefit of the doubt and decide they may have considered it more important that he get off to a good start with his new mother.

"We went SwissAir, and they were great because they're used to it. So they gave chocolate to him, and there were a couple of other adoptive parents on there and they were very nice to him. He had no problem on the plane. He was touching everything. I mean as long as you give Caleb what he wants, he's all right. It's when you start *not* giving him what he wants that he gets feisty.

"He was exactly like he is now," Golda says, "touching everything, always into things. He was rocking. He would go to anybody. I remember going to Kinko's and there was some guy there and Caleb held up his arms, open wide. That's what he did when he wanted to get picked up or held. He only had four words. He used to feel so frustrated that he couldn't talk that he would bite you."

"I've heard that sometimes children who come from an orphanage have problems sleeping when they get here. Did he have any sleep problems?" I ask.

"No, Caleb always slept. He went right to sleep at seven o'clock every night. In his orphanage he would sleep twelve hours a day, at least. Sixteen hours. They're on schedules: get up and eat, go back to bed, very structured. But now he has sleep issues. He wants to sleep in my bed all the time. Sometimes he'll sleep in his bed, but he wants to sleep with somebody. He never had food issues—always ate great. It's just learning problems; it's just learning. But he was breastfed, too. The breastfeeding, the good relationship in the orphanage—that helped.

"So I took him to the doctor that specializes in international adoptions. She said, 'This kid has issues.' I said, 'What do you mean?' She said, 'You have a new job. You're an advocate for your son.' I said, 'What do you mean?' She said, 'You better get him into services right now.' So I said, 'OK.'

"The doctor kind of scared me. She didn't do it intentionally. She just said it, and I kind of took her seriously. I figured she must know. Then I called two agencies for early intervention, and I went to one and they evaluated him as age appropriate. So I said, 'I don't think he's age appropriate.' They didn't understand international adoptions at that point. So I got speech therapy for him, but first they were going to put him in a group. He needed more intensive services, so I got someone to work with him individually. And I took Caleb to the guru in occupational therapy. She goes to Romania every year and works in the orphanages, and she evaluated him at one point, and he wasn't the worst case they've seen, but he's not the best case, either.

"He's always gone back to see that doctor. She looks at him as an adopted child, and to her, he's doing great. To me, he's not doing great, so it was hard. Because I never banked on a kid with special needs."

Golda has come a long way since she said "I am not interested in a special needs kid; I can't do it." She's gathering information from the experts, making informed decisions, and fighting to make sure Caleb gets what he needs.

"And the reason I chose private school was because the first neuropsych evaluation that was done said he needed a small, language-based classroom and there was none. The public school wanted to put him in a kindergarten with thirty-two kids. And I said no. It's almost like you have a sense as a parent—my kid's not going to be doing well there. So that's why I did Touchstone. And it's hard because he's almost seven and he's still not reading."

"I think he's making good progress," I say. "His language is improving. I can understand him more of the time."

"He is, but on the other hand, you say as a parent he should be like all the other kids. It's just a feeling; it's not my thinking. But still the end result is that all these things that we do with him are going to make a difference to him when he's an adult. If you don't do them, what they say is that he won't get to where he needs to be. These kids have to have issues. I mean, Eastern Europe, there's no prenatal care. I mean his mother was sixteen. I'm sure she smoked; she probably drank. I'm sure she probably didn't eat right. When his brain was developing, what was going on? You know what someone said to me? She said, 'Think of it as if they have a file cabinet. And when an infant is born, things are put into their file cabinet. Well, these kids' file drawers are blank and you have to go back and put things in.'

"But if he hadn't been taken from the orphanage, he would have been dead. He would have been a male prostitute. There's no doubt in my mind. If he hadn't been adopted he would have gone from that orphanage to the bigger orphanage. You know Caleb and I know Caleb. What would he have done? He would have been with those twelve-year-olds—'Let's run away today!' What would have happened? He would have run away. In the subways, my brother said, they're all prostitutes, kid prostitutes, and they are living in the subways and they're living in the sewers. Caleb would have been a prime candidate because he's so cute. So he would have been dead. Maybe that's the reason that they got him out of there so quick, too, because they knew the kid should not go to the big orphanage.

"It's been a long road," Golda says. "I just want him to feel good about himself."

"And it's not over yet," I say, thinking that even after he learns to read, school will continue to be challenging for him.

"It's never over," she says. "You know that; you're a mother."

* 3 *

All Alone

Katya is at the sand table with Lily. Soon Lily's voice interrupts me at the nearby art table, where I am teaching Shawn the intricacies of going over-under-over-under on the paper placemat he's weaving. "I want these animals to be nice!" Lily complains, pointing to the two brown plastic foxes in Katya's hands and the one small fox in her own. Lily sees that she has my attention. "And Katya won't let me use that board!" She points to a wooden board that spans the width of the sandbox, serving as a road, a bridge, or a place to put extra toys. Katya has pulled it over to her side of the box, so Lily can barely reach it if she stretches.

"So, there are two problems," I say. "One is that the board is not in the middle. The second is that Lily wants the foxes to be nicer foxes . . . I'm going to hold the animals while we talk about this," I add, as Katya ignores my words and continues with her play.

Once I am holding the mother and baby foxes, she moves the board a couple of centimeters toward the center. "I moved it back," she mutters.

"Lily, is that OK now?" I ask.

Lily shakes her head no. "And I want to pretend the baby fox was a little too close to the edge and she fell in," she adds.

"I *said* you could do that," Katya tells her.

"But I wanted it to be an accident and the mommy *did* save her," Lily explains. "And Katya has the mommy fox and a baby fox besides, and I only have one baby fox."

I expect most of the girls in the class, playing mother and baby foxes, would agree with Lily: if the baby fox falls over the edge, it should be an accident and the mommy should save her. But Katya's early experiences were different than theirs.

Some orphanages in Russia have far less than fifty cents a day to feed each child,[1] and many newly arrived international adoptees from Russia are underweight and under height and have small head circumferences, a serious sign of malnutrition.[2] If this was Katya's experience, then her early life would not have taught her that the world is trustworthy. The psychologist Erik Erikson called this first stage of development, from age zero to two years, "Trust vs. Mistrust." It's the time when a child should learn that the world is trustworthy, that her needs will be met, and that she can count on other people to love and care for her.[3]

Yet for Katya, the mother fox might not be counted on to rescue the baby; the baby fox must be prepared to save herself.

"So what are you going to do?" I ask the girls.

"We could each move to a different place," Lily suggests, "away from each other." She gets up to leave the game. Her mother has been encouraging her to move away from Katya when she feels Katya is being mean to her, rather than coming home and crying about it.

"Do you want to do that?" I ask. "Or do you want to work this out?"

"I want to work this out," Lily decides. "I like sand."

"I want to move," Katya says immediately.

"So you can't even agree about that," I say.

"That's a funny argument," Lily says, laughing.

"It's because I didn't have any breakfast," Katya says abruptly. "That's why I'm doing this."

"Why don't you try eating and see if that helps?" I say. Usually any suggestion that I want her to eat is rejected, but since the idea came from her, maybe she'll follow through with it.

---

1. Miller, *Handbook of International Adoption Medicine*, 54.

2. Ibid., 159.

3. Erik H. Erikson, *Childhood and Society* (New York: W. W. Norton, 1950).

"No!" she says. "I don't want to."

I decide to attend to Shawn, who has been adding paper strips the wrong way while I have been talking to Katya. "Every time you went over with the first strip, you're going to go under with the new one," I show him. Maybe Katya will eat while I'm not looking.

"Katya! Stop! You'll get sand in my eyes," I hear Lily say.

"I'm just brushing sand off the board," Katya answers.

Lily gets up and starts brushing the sand off her hands, looking as though she's going to leave the sandbox.

"We could play in sand and be nice to each other," I hear Katya tell her. "And you could be two foxes."

Lily does not answer.

"What's your idea to do?" Katya persists, eager to compromise now. She knows what it would take to convince Lily to stay in the game with her, but it is too late. Lily has gone to the Lego table to see what Elisabeth is playing there.

"Then who will play with me?" Katya says quietly. "It's raining, it's pouring," she sings, loudly enough for Lily to hear. "The old man is snoring." She adds a little volume when no one notices. "He bumped his head and went to bed and he couldn't get up in the morning," she continues, sprinkling sand over the mother and baby foxes.

"What'll I do?" she says quietly to me. "I'm all alone."

* 4 *

Gray Days in Russia

I sit in Robert and Lynn's house a few weeks later, sinking into their soft brown couch and hearing the story of their trip to Russia to adopt Katya. Robert turns on a video that was sent to them from the orphanage when they first heard she would be available for adoption. I recognize a look around the eyes and mouth as I watch a thin, twenty-month-old Katya in a starched red dress toddle around a shabby room. Robert explains that this room is used only for making videos to send to potential adoptive families. At one point a caregiver puts an arm around Katya and she smiles.

Lynn and Robert had taken the video to a doctor specializing in international adoptions, who told them that she looked relatively healthy and that the smile was a good sign. So after a lot of paperwork, they flew to Russia, then drove two hours from Moscow to her orphanage. They walked up a flight of stairs and into a dim, gray, room.

"It felt like it was something from one of those dark movies from the fifties," Lynn says. The floor-to-ceiling windows were frosted, and the institution had a bug problem so they were sealed shut.

Robert continues the story. "There was a long hallway. It was dimly lit and did not have windows. Off that hallway were these big, big, big dormitory rooms. In Katya's room there were about twenty-four beds and they're all lined up in rows, steel-framed beds, children's size, no box springs, just a thin mattress right on the frame. Immaculate—I mean really, really clean. Very bare, no rugs, no pictures on the walls. Nothing. Beds in rows. And then to the far left as you went into the room, there were a number of red plastic potties, enough for however many kids were in that room.

And they're all lined up in a row, and all the kids are sitting on them all at the same time, screaming and crying and miserable. And the kids couldn't get off until they'd had a bowel movement. It was clear to me the kids had been on there way too long. And there were one or two people overseeing this. I want to say one."

Robert opens a thick notebook and reads from an entry in their diary from the trip. They had played with Katya, and then they walked up a big flight of stairs to the room where she was going to be fed. Katya was doing fine. Her caretaker held one hand as she climbed the adult-sized stairs. "When we started walking toward the room that she eats in, for some reason that we didn't understand, she threw herself on the floor face down and her arms and legs were flailing and she was screeching uncontrollably. And again, they weren't being mean but they just had to keep to their schedule and they weren't especially patient. They didn't hurt her or anything, but they just picked her up and said things like 'She can be very stubborn.' Lynn speaks and understands Russian," he explains. "It was very alarming because we didn't have any kids who had ever had temper tantrums to know what they were even like, so we were, of course, wondering what was wrong with our kid."

They were taken into an adjoining room, where there were wooden child-sized tables and chairs along one wall and there was a white kitchenette. Robert continues, "This is where they sat us down and fed Katya with us. And they force-fed her. I mean they were just jamming stuff in her mouth until she threw up."

Now I can imagine that Katya had known where they were headed when she threw the tantrum.

"It was like broth, bread, and some sort of kefir," Lynn says. "And the woman was shoving it in her mouth so fast that Katya knew how to clear her throat from choking very early on. And it was horrible. She would regurgitate it. It was just because they didn't have enough time per child; they had to just keep it going. Not that they were being cruel."

"Imagine if you had to get twenty-four kids fed and very few of them feed themselves," Robert says. "We watched one of her caretakers feed her in less than two minutes.

"Well, this is very much what it's like trying to get her to eat today. She stalls and delays and starts problems where there aren't problems, and it's a big cajoling process unless she's really, really hungry."

I picture Katya looking angrily in her lunchbox each day when we sit down to eat, complaining about whatever she finds there, even though I know Robert and Lynn try to give her the food she likes best. How long will it take for Katya to discover that eating can be enjoyable, though her early experiences with food were full of misery?

"And then they had to get them cleaned up," Lynn adds. "And then get them changed. And they all had some form of diarrhea because giardia is ubiquitous there. So they probably were on those potties many times a day. What they basically did was time intervals between when they ate and when they stuck them on the potty."

"They didn't want to wash the diapers?" I ask.

"They probably didn't have time. They tried to do the best they could."

After Lynn and Robert had visited Katya for five days, they were able to bring her to an apartment where they were staying with a family.

"Although it was a lot nicer than the orphanage, Katya was clearly freaked out by the change. There was a lot of screaming and crying of a whole different nature," Lynn says. "Like her brain was saying, 'This isn't right; I want to go home.'"

"Then the real nightmare was the airplane," Robert continues. "Now think about it—she had never ridden in a car."

Katya had probably never been outdoors since the first five or six months, when she was with her mother. Robert and Lynn had heard that her mother would take her carriage out and leave her on the street and the neighbors would take care of her. "We don't know if that's true, about her mother," Robert says. "But between, say, six months and a year and eleven months, she was indoors all the time."

"Unless you really have an understanding of what's been going on in Russia for the past fifty years," he explains, "you can't grasp it. There are PhDs living on the street. The judge in the adoption court was not being paid. The economy is so bad that people who would be making $200,000 here are living on the street there. The director at the orphanage is probably the only one there who gets paid. Most of the people working there are volunteers. So you get a twenty-year-old person who never had a job period—I mean that's a given, that's why prostitution rings are so huge there. That's why people go to Russia to enslave children or women. They're just all on the street. And it's been a very prolonged cycle. It's horrible."

Lynn and Robert describe how they took Katya outdoors, drove her in a car to a hotel, stayed there for a couple of days, put her in another car, and drove her to the airport. There were sights and sounds she'd never heard before. They got in an airplane, with its strange pressure changes.

"Literally, we had seventeen hours of crying, kicking, biting, and screaming," Robert says. "She did not fall asleep for seventeen hours. She bloodied me, she scratched my face, she scratched my eyes, she bit me multiple times hard enough to draw blood. At one point I took her back to this hallway at the back of the plane between two galleys, and one of the flight attendants helped me fill it with a bunch of pillows and blankets and we put her down, expecting that she would be so exhausted that she would pass out and fall asleep. She didn't. She flailed in there for a couple of hours and screamed and cried."

When they finally arrived home, they sat her on her high chair and made her Cream of Wheat. The first thing she did was to pull the bowl close to herself.

"In case somebody was going to take it away," Robert explains.

"And she ate three servings all really fast," Lynn continues. "And it took about six months for her to become a normal, finicky child."

"Now she doesn't want to eat unless she's really hungry," Robert says. "So to me there's a really strong connection with the orphanage and all her eating behaviors; none of them have ever been comfortable eating behaviors, from my point of view."

Katya had been tiny when they first saw her—twenty-one pounds at twenty-two months, and very short. When they first took her to the doctor, her height and weight were below where the chart began for her age, so low they weren't even listed as possibilities.

"She was literally skin and bones," Lynn says. "The other thing I recall when she first came home was all she wanted to eat was bananas and raw vegetables. She wanted carrots and cauliflower, raw. She wanted anything crunchy. It's almost like her body was screaming for this.

"But now," she adds, "I don't think the eating thing is really different than a lot of parents that I talk to about their kids. I don't see anything that says this is an atypical situation. And she also manages to leave food on her plate, which I think is a good sign, instead of eating it all up."

Robert goes into the kitchen and brings out a bowl of blackberries, blueberries, and grapes. We munch silently for a few minutes, in a brief respite from the pain of Katya's story.

"There's another thing she's just outgrowing," Lynn says. "She would be with us on a train or on a vacation, go up to a perfect stranger, and put her arm around his leg. She'd say, 'Mine.' When she was older, we had to sit down and explain to her, give her the rules of the world. She would be the kind of kid who would just go with anyone. Easily. 'Help me find my puppy?' 'Sure.' You don't have to bribe her with food. I don't know if that's a neediness thing. It's as if she feels like 'Strangers aren't strangers to me. They're just people I don't know yet.' We had to teach her fear of strangers, instead of it being a natural sense.

"But the biggest thing we had to go through with Katya," Lynn says, "our nightmare experience, lasted until she was easily four."

If the force-feeding and the airplane trip were not their biggest trauma, I am not sure I'm ready to hear.

"When she would wake up from a nap," Lynn continues, unaware of my reluctance to listen, "she was somewhere else, and it went anywhere from a twenty-minute experience to a two-hour experience, just screaming like someone was going to kill her. And we tried hugging her, we tried holding her, we tried waking her up slowly, we tried letting her wake up on her own. One thing that was successful was when a little kid next door came over and he woke her up. She was crying, and he went up to her crib and he said, 'Hi, Katya,' and then she saw him and she smiled. And that was the one time she had a pleasant waking-up experience for about a year.

"It seemed to be worse when it was from a nap than when it was from a full night's sleep. But even when she'd wake up in the morning, it was horrible. If it happened in the car, if she fell asleep when I picked her up from day care, I would have to sometimes leave the windows or the doors open, or sit there with the heat on, depending on the time of year, until it was over. I couldn't get her out of the car seat. I had bloody noses. She chipped my tooth. It was horrible."

This lasted for almost two years, all the way through day care.

"Was it the same at day care, after nap time?" I ask.

"There she would be fine," Robert says. "When she woke up there were a bunch of other sounds going on, chirping of kids. She would get off the mat and all the kids were playing, and when she walked around she'd be playing with the other kids."

I picture Katya at the orphanage, surrounded by rows of hard beds, and wonder if those children chirped when they woke up. Did they offer a form of toddler comfort to one another?

"I wonder if having other kids around is reassuring to her," I say. "It's intimacy that frightens her, because then she is afraid of losing the person she loves."

"That feels really, really right," Robert says. "That bit about having lots of kids around when she wakes up, that really feels like it connects. And the screaming got better as she got older; it happened less frequently and for shorter periods."

"She still has that neediness to like sit on you, say, 'Mine, I want you, I need you, you're mine,'" Lynn says. "I mean it's decreasing, but she still has this need for physical closeness, an incredible amount of contact. We believe in the family bed, so Katya can choose to stay in her bed or come and crawl in with us, and go back and forth if she wants, but I think this kid would be miserable in a family where she couldn't crawl into bed and snuggle up with her parents, unless there was another kid in the family and she could jump in their bed.

"I still think there's this fear, on her part, when I leave her. When

I was leaving this morning, she gave me this scared look, like I'm not going to come back, she's not going to see me, and I said, 'I'm picking you up this afternoon.' It's not like a manipulative look. She shot me this look of fear.

"Now when she goes to sleep, she often stays in her own bed for the whole night. But if she does wake up to go to the bathroom, she'll dive into our bed. And usually she grabs my hand—and she's been doing this since she was a baby: she grabs it, she clutches it, and she pulls it to herself and she is breaking my hand. And then I'll give her hand a kiss and she'll relax a little bit. But I will always wake up with my arm wrapped around her neck or her arm wrapped around my neck, pulling me to her. It's really intense and she'll still do it. She'll grab my hand and stroke my hand.

"There is something called night terrors," Lynn adds, "and I don't know what that is, but it was a terror for me.

"There's a whole bunch of things that whenever we hit a snag we say we wonder how much of this is related to Katya being Katya and how much is related to environmental problems and we're never going to know.

"But now it's just like there is a whole different kid here. I still get the chills all over, several times a day, whether I'm with her or merely thinking about her, when I think about what could have become of her had she stayed in Russia and what she has become here—a vivacious child who lives life to the fullest."

∗ 5 ∗

Jasper's First Stories

Jasper is the youngest child in the class. He just turned five, but he can decode any print he sees, and in tiny, well-formed letters, he writes words that are spelled perfectly. At playtime, while Caleb, Shawn, and Glen drive motorcycles to Boston in the block area, rob the girls' house in the doll corner, and turn their motorcycles into a pirate ship with a plank, Jasper sits silently at a small table, practicing the alphabet in uppercase, lowercase, and cursive. When I glance at him to see if he's secretly watching the nearby action, I never catch him at it. He appears focused on his lists.

"Do you want to tell a story?" I ask quietly, sitting down next to him.

"Yes," he whispers. Jasper does want to tell a story, but he does not seem to know what it might be. After a long pause, which I am determined not to break, he says, "Spot." He leans closer to watch while I write the word in his notebook.

There is another long pause. His dark eyes look slowly around the room, stopping at the art table, where three girls are decorating boxes with ribbon for puppy homes.

"Ribbon," Jasper adds. After another long pause, he presents me with a full sentence: "Jasper is Spot and his dog is Blue. The end." During the next pause I consider the possibility of suggesting action. If Jasper is imagining he is the dog's owner, he could walk the dog or feed it. If he's pretending he's a dog, he and Blue could run and play chase. "The television," Jasper says, as though the words "The end" have no more meaning than the "A, B, C" on his paper. I try to make my face as immobile as his, so my disappointment does not show. I had hoped that Spot and his dog might turn into an understandable plot. "They turn it off," he adds.

Jasper's gaze returns to his paper, where he begins to write "Monday, Tuesday, Wednesday."

With all his skills in reading and writing, I worry about the empty place where his stories might be. I decide to pretend he has told a story, and when we act it out I provide some missing links. I direct the dog to bark and the television to be loud and Jasper to turn it off.

The next week, I am pleased to see that Jasper has written his own name on the list of children waiting to tell stories. When it is his turn, he begins more quickly.

"There's a truck." That's a fine beginning; all the boys could relate to it as a good place to start, with a wide range of possible actions that could follow.

But Jasper puts his head down and mumbles something that sounds like "carambals." "What did you say?" I ask. "It's hard to hear you when your head is down like that." He looks at me briefly, a tiny smile at the corners of his mouth.

"Stuck. Karate guys."

"What does that mean?" I ask, disappointed at the unintelligible jumble of sounds. Is he embarrassed that he made a mistake—said something I could not understand—and is now trying to cover it up? I'm reminded of sitting at the dining-room table, the youngest child in my family, saying something that unexpectedly makes everyone laugh, and then pretending I had done it on purpose.

The tiny smile makes its fleeting appearance. "That means the truck is smaller," Jasper explains unexpectedly. "There's a big one, too. That's the end."

When we act out the story, Jasper chooses to be the small truck and Elisabeth takes the role of the big one. If Caleb, Shawn, or Glen had told such a story, any of them would surely have chosen to be the larger truck, speeding around the rug that is our stage.

But Jasper holds an imaginary steering wheel and moves slowly, silently but proudly, behind Elisabeth around the perimeter of the rug. "The little one doesn't drive faster," he announces. They return to their places, satisfied with the two characters and the single piece of action that connects them.

✳ 6 ✳

Lucky Boy, Lucky Boy

I sit in my classroom at my usual spot at the story table, but instead of hearing about a puppy house or a mother and baby deer, I'm listening as Jasper's mother, Gwen, tells me the story of his adoption from Cambodia.

"In January I got a fax at work," she says. "Basically it just said no hepatitis, no syphilis, no HIV. And there was a picture." She opens a book of photographs and shows me his passport. "Kingdom of Cambodia," it announces in English across the page in a graceful line of swirls and circles that is reminiscent of the alphabet in an old Bible.

"That is his Pali name, Vireak Both. It means 'brave son.' It's pronounced 'Vi-wreck'-but.'" Jasper's eyes stare out of the picture, huge and frightened; his mouth is open in alarm. "Then they say, 'Do you want this baby?' He was three months old. That was in January."

She turns the page and we see Jasper at four months. "Here's the picture they sent us later, after we agreed," she says. "Chubby. Look at those rolls of fat on his knees." Together we admire the healthy-looking baby with skin the color of milky cocoa. "The social worker wrote, 'He's a keeper.'

"The physician at the orphanage is actually a pediatrician from Boston. She got involved in international adoptions and she moved to Cambodia. She had a nurse that she worked with, and one of them would be here and one would be there at all times. I would be constantly calling the nurse and I'd say, 'I got a picture of Jasper, he's got a bump on his head.' She'd say, 'That's a bug bite.' Every time I would call and say, 'I'm worried about Vireak Both,' and they would say, 'Vireak Both, he's fine,' because he was such a quiet, easy baby. And he was just kind of going with the flow.

"So I got a lot of e-mail communication from the doctor saying 'He's OK, I checked on him.' So that really helped because I was afraid he'd have malaria or some bizarre disease."

"And was that information accurate?" I ask. "He actually was healthy?"

"It was very accurate. So in January we got the referral, and in February we got the pictures. And we were supposed to go over in February, but then there was a political problem and they held us up until April. It was horrible for us. Every day we didn't know if we could go."

"He looks great in those pictures," I say, thinking of the video of Katya, so thin in her starched red dress.

"This woman is his nanny, Kunthea. It's pronounced Coon-tee-ah." Gwen's voice gets gentle and soft as she points to the picture of a smiling woman who looks lovingly at Jasper while holding him up for the picture. "And one of the interesting things about this orphanage is that there's one child, one nanny. They have a maximum of two infants per nanny, and if either child has any kind of special needs or health issues, it's a maximum of one infant to a nanny. And they're assigned full time. The nannies are young women who in many cases lost their families through land mines or whatever. Some have their own children, and they had a school at the orphanage where those children were taught sewing. The nannies were provided with room and board in return for raising these infants. Kunthea adored him—she cried when we took him away."

"Is this typical of Cambodia?" I ask.

"You know, I think so, because when we came back we took him to a doctor that specializes in international adoptions, and she examined Jasper and everything was great and she said to us, 'You know, Cambodia knows how to do it right. I see these kids all the time, and I wish I could send the rest of the world to Cambodia to see what they're doing.'"

I can understand now why Gwen had felt that I was prejudging Jasper at our first conference, that I was assuming all international adoptions were the same. Gwen had worked hard to ensure that her baby would have had the best possible care as an infant. Katya's experience of being force-fed was very different from Jasper's loving care by Kunthea. And children who come from foster families, as many internationally adopted children do, would have had a whole different variety of experiences.

"And then we went, finally. This is a picture of his orphanage." She shows a picture of a tiny house on stilts with a three-tiered roof and a red, yellow, blue, and green striped awning over the entrance. "All the babies slept in baskets hanging from the ceiling."

"How many orphans were there?"

"Eight, when we were there. But I think they could take up to twenty. The house is on stilts because the water rises in the winter. They would keep this shady spot underneath the house in the summer so the kids could be outside there."

"So they got to play outside?" I ask.

"They got to play outside like normal kids. The inside of the orphanage was spotless. Wooden planked floors, but completely spotless, and all the children when we got there were sitting on the floor, and they had some kind of blocks and sticks and little round rocks and things that they'd be playing with. The three- and four-year-olds would be playing with the littlest ones with an adult involved, so it looked like day care. They had a space outside where the older children were playing the equivalent of soccer or kickball, running around. Outside the orphanage when we got there, they had a water pump that they had recently built, so they did have fresh water, and they were trying to get a filter system, which they now have. But when we were in Cambodia, you would go down the street and they were selling Coke bottles of water everywhere, and the water was the color of Coke. The water was not something you'd want to drink.

"We chose Cambodia purposefully, because we had heard good things about it. Our agency told us in November they had babies there as young as three weeks and they were available for placement immediately. So we said, 'Fine, we'll go.' And literally we filled out the paperwork and had there not been a political coup, we could have had a baby in five weeks. And because it was turning over so fast, these children were not languishing in an orphanage. They told us there are baby boys in Cambodia that are available quickly; you have to agree to adopt a boy, because the boys outnumber the girls three to one."

"Why are there only boys?" I ask.

"I understand that at one time there were both boys and girls available for adoption, but when we went over, that wasn't the case. We heard lots of different possible reasons for the surplus of boys. A lot of people who were waiting to adopt were looking at China, so they had their hearts set on having girls. So that might have led to a lesser demand for boys. Some people told us that there were more boys available because the eldest girl in a family stays to care for her parents when she gets married, so a girl is needed. Others told us that boys and men are thought to be lazy and unproductive, so they are not considered as helpful growing up. And in Cambodia, school costs money. In most families, only boys go to school. So boys are expensive."

Gwen's voice gets so quiet I have to lean forward to hear her. "And then there's the reason we heard most often: girls can be sold into sex or slave trades. So there are lots of unwanted boys. I guess it's the opposite of China's situation in this regard.

"So we said we would go get a boy, that's fine. But today they do not allow international adoptions from Cambodia because of allegations that people were buying babies to sell for adoption. So now these children are three, four or five; they're building preschools for them, the infants are still coming in. They're going to be overcrowded and turning kids away. They'll be out on the streets. As it is, at seven you can't be in an orphanage any more. At seven you're considered grown and you can now be independent. I look at Jasper now—they'd say, 'In two years you're an adult.' He can't make his own peanut butter sandwich. I don't know how they're supposed to survive."

"What do you know about his origins?" I ask.

"That's where it gets tricky. When we got there, we met with the orphanage director, and she told us that that Jasper's birth mother was married to someone who had an alcohol problem and that he had beaten her severely and that she'd gone into labor in the hospital. She was nine months, but she had delivered because of the beating. A social worker at the hospital had talked with her and had convinced her that she should place this baby for adoption because she had a violent home and several other children. And whether she lived or died we didn't know. They said she was beaten badly enough that she could have died. But she placed the baby at birth, so the social worker brought Jasper to the orphanage. That's what we were told. That's why when we went over, we were so grateful to these people.

"When we got there, he was six months. The orphanage director gave us the formula, and she had the translator say, 'And he also likes pork, rice, fish, and bananas.' And I thought, 'At six months?' And when we went to the restaurant later he *was* eating everything—pork, rice, fish, no problem."

"So his nanny had only one other baby to take care of?" I ask.

"She only had Jasper. But the rule is they can have two. She was with him all day and all night. The first time we saw him, my thought was, we were going to go and take him away from his nanny and he was going to be hysterical. And he just came right to us. He was not crying, he was not upset, he was totally comfortable, and the doctor had said that was part of the way the nannies are there—they're not their mother, they're their nanny, and they're very aware of that. They didn't papoose them and things like that so they couldn't separate. He separated easily. I was so afraid of attachment disorder—that was my biggest fear—but the doctor here said she hasn't seen it in Cambodian kids; they learn how to connect, and Jasper connected to me instantly. He bonded to me. He's much closer to David now, but when he was little he was totally mine, 100 percent.

"We don't know if that's his real story or not. But that's what we were told. If we go to a Cambodian restaurant, they'll say, 'Oh, beautiful child,' and we say, 'He's from Phnom Penh.' And they would always say, 'Oh, no, no, Laos. Laotian child.' So he may well be partly Laotian. We don't know where he came from or what he did. He's very, very light skinned, too, for the Cambodian children. The true Khmer children are darker skinned than Jasper. But the borders to

Thailand and Laos are so close. It would make sense that people have come and gone."

"But you do know that he was brought at day one to the orphanage, so it's not like he had some terrible history, right?" I ask.

"We know that at three months he was in the orphanage, because that's when we got the picture. We were told he was brought there at day one, but if that's a lie then he could have been doing just about anything for three months. We don't know where he came from at that point."

"Except that he was pretty healthy at three months—he was chubby."

"He was being fed, that's for sure. He ate everything; he was a very good eater."

Gwen turns to the next pages of photos. "This is right after we got him. His motor coordination is good for six months—he's pushing himself up. He was rolling over. So he was right where he should have been."

"What was it like coming home?" I ask.

"Coming home was wonderful. Everybody was so welcoming and excited and happy to have him here."

"Was he OK on the airplane?" I ask, remembering Lynn and Robert's flight with Katya.

"He slept the entire way. It was thirty-five hours, and he was awake for about an hour and fifteen minutes. And they had told us to get the bulkhead seat and put the child on the floor. The vibration usually puts them to sleep, and we were dreading it completely, and he got on the plane and slept the whole way. Thirty-five hours. So when he came home his sleep cycle was pretty normal. He wasn't reverse timed or anything, because we just lost a day but our days and nights were in synch, and so he did fine with that. We had a baby mill, and whatever we ate we just ground it up—forget the whole pediatrician one-food-at-a-time thing. So whatever we had, you know, lasagna, throw it in there; he ate everything. And no problems.

"When we went over, we brought one suitcase with our clothes and Jasper's clothes and one entire suitcase of donations. We were told what to bring. We brought vitamins with iron, and all of these children get a multivitamin every day. We were told to bring the powdered Pedialyte because if they get diarrhea it's fatal. And then all kinds of other things that they need like Neosporin and lice shampoo and medication for scabies. A lot of the children did have scabies when we came over. We also were told a lot of them might have difficulty adjusting to the food and might end up having diarrhea. But Jasper didn't have a touch of scabies. He had nothing. So we were lucky.

"The one thing he did have, though, and to this day, and this is why I hedge when you say that we know the first three months were great—Jasper had night terrors, horrible night terrors. It was very freaky because he was six, seven months old and he would wake up, open his eyes, and scream like someone was poking him with a hot poker. And he would be sitting up and just screaming his eyes out, and we literally just picked him up, we took him out in the rain, we had him out in the snow, we would turn all the lights on, we did everything to try to wake him up, because he would not wake up and he would scream, it was horrible."

"Was it like that every night?" I ask.

"It wasn't. It was about once a week. And in day care it happened three times. All three times he woke up from a nap in the middle of the day, and they would call me because they just couldn't calm him down. They didn't know what to do, and he was not awake. And when he woke up he was happy and fine and doing his thing. But when it happened, you basically could do nothing but hold him and just let him scream until he woke up.

"Somewhere about the age of one and a half to two he stopped and it never happened again. But Jasper still has a sleep disorder. And he always has. He doesn't sleep at all. I mean Jasper sleeps about four or five hours a night on a good night, and he's not tired."

"So is that a disorder?" I ask.

"I think it is now, because he can't sleep even when he wants to. I mean Jasper will very often go to bed at 8:00, and he will fall asleep somewhere around midnight. And now that he's getting older, on weekends he will sleep on his own until 8:30, so that tells me that he needs about eight hours of sleep but he can't put himself to sleep. He can't turn it off. And he's also been a kid who needs light and sound. He can't be in total quiet."

"Did he sleep with his nanny?" I ask, wondering if his difficulty going to sleep began with the loss of that close relationship.

"The nanny slept in the same room—it was one big room—but he slept in the basket by himself. So he didn't sleep next to a person. We made a decision early on that we were not co-sleeping, we were putting him in his own bed, so we did that and it wasn't really a problem, he adjusted to that OK. He wasn't a child that had trouble in his room. Jasper never woke up crying, either. He woke up and just played with his fingers or whatever he had. And you'd walk in there panicky, thinking something was wrong, and he's just sitting there, happy as a clam, when he woke up. He was in day care with someone who's been doing daycare for twenty-three years, and she'd never seen anything like his night terrors."

"But they didn't tell you he was having these in the orphanage?" I ask.

"No. They would have thought that we would judge them, think that it was their fault, that they had done something bad to him."

As Gwen's story turns darker, I wonder how often I give parents enough time to describe the strengths of their family and their child before I expect them to discuss what worries them.

She continues. "And we thought Phnom Penh was the most disturbing place we've ever been in our lives. When we were there, they told us that it was not safe for us to leave the hotel. So we were in a beautiful hotel, and we were there for five days waiting to get a flight out, and we thought we'd see a little of the country. We didn't want to go too far with a new baby, so the orphanage director gave us a guide who went with us everywhere we went, just like a bodyguard. And he took us around the city so we could see things. We went into the bazaar to go souvenir shopping. And we saw so many children, so many children, running around naked with deformities. We saw children running around with huge hernias in their abdomens, naked, begging for money. Almost all the adults were land mine victims. Almost nobody had four limbs. They were on crutches and whatever. The children were swarming around. They were either missing limbs or they had cuts and disease, and they were very sickly looking, and then we saw this one woman. I can still see it, this old woman. I thought she was spitting up blood because this red stuff was pouring out of her mouth, and I completely lost it. I almost had a panic attack. I mean literally, David and the guide had to carry me out of there. I was holding Jasper so close to me. Everyone wanted to touch him. They would all say, 'Lucky boy, lucky boy,' and then they would touch him."

"Because you had him?" I ask.

"Because I had him. Because he was leaving. And everywhere we went people thanked us. They would say, 'Thank you. Lucky boy, lucky boy.' No one was aggressive, but they all wanted to touch him. And I was holding him against me, and I didn't want these people to touch him. And so David and the driver got me out of there, and I was crying and crying. I was in the cab, I couldn't even breathe, I was so upset, and I remember this little boy running up to the cab, and he had a big hernia and he was with that old woman who was spitting up the blood, and I just thought it was so horrible. And it turned out it was a ritual and she was eating berries and spitting up the juice. Eventually the cab driver managed to explain this to us, but all I saw was a child and his grandmother dying with an ulcer or something, spitting up blood.

"I think that kids with any kind of problem just get turned out into the street. So if they have a cleft lip, they have a hernia when they're born, which is fairly common—anything like that, they just turn them out in the street. Because they're unadoptable, they can't treat them. And right now the spread of AIDS is so rampant. Tons of kids are on the street because their parents died. Roteang Orphanage was started to help the babies and kids with HIV and AIDS, but they have only the ones who are brought in by their parents who are dying. There are so many others that are just out there, and they're all HIV positive and there's no treatment, there's no cocktail, there's no anything.

"The country itself, if you go into the museums or any of the mosques, the artwork is incredible. You can just see what a rich country it was before the Khmer Rouge, but now it's awful.

"There's a lot to understand about where these kids come from, I think. Even if they come from a perfect loving environment, like Jasper did, the adults who are around them are heartsick. It's like being raised by a parent who's depressed.

"I don't know what happened to him before he wound up with us, but I think that psychologically there has to be an impact, if nothing else, to taking him away from that nanny who was there doing so much for him, and the night terrors were part of that. Jasper's doing great. He was like the healthiest, happy kid you could ever see in your life, but I think there was still an unhealed wound of some kind, and it's manifest in his night terrors."

Part Two

*

Stories, Rules,
and Land Mines

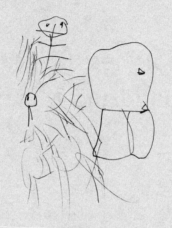

* 7 *

The Mama Business

"I have one important thing to tell you," I announce at morning meeting. "After recess, we're going to have a special all-school assembly."

"Mama, Mama," Katya squeals, pretending to be alarmed at my statement. Everyone laughs with her.

Recently, at my suggestion, Katya's parents consulted a social worker with a practice specializing in adopted children. Robert and Lynn were concerned about some of Katya's difficult behavior at home — problems around food and around routines. I was looking for suggestions for dealing with her disruptive behavior in school and her need to manipulate her friends, two issues that seemed to revolve around her need to always be the center of attention.

The social worker recommended a book called *1-2-3 Magic: Effective Discipline for Children 2–12* by Thomas Phelan, and suggested that we all implement the behavior management plan it described in order to have an approach that was consistent between home and school. According to the book, we should explain to Katya what the behavior was that she had to stop and then give her two warnings, counting simply, "one" the first time and "two" the second, with no further discussion about it. If we got to "three," she would have a five-minute time-out at a table alone, where she could color quietly until the timer went off. Then she could return to her previous activity.

I don't like to use behavior management plans and time-outs. I believe they cut off the discussions in which children can learn to understand other people's points of view and learn about the effects of their behavior on their friends. I find that behavior management plans teach children to behave in ways that enable them to avoid being caught and to tattle on others as often as possible. When, instead of a time-out, I have a discussion with the children involved with the problem, I often find the conflict or issue was more complex than I had realized—other children were also involved, there were misunderstandings or confusions, and my original idea of what happened may not have been correct. Usually, a full discussion elicits plans so that we can avoid the problem in the future and helps children see that any situation has many different points of view.

With Katya I have an additional concern: will she experience the time-out as one more abandonment, like the rejection by her mother who may have left her on the street in her carriage or the abandonment by the volunteers in the orphanage who had no time to meet her needs?

Brenda McCreight, author of *Parenting Your Adopted Older Child*,[1] suggests that it is better for children with issues around attachment to have a time-out in the same room as the adult, rather than being isolated. I set up a "time-in" place that is out of sight of the children when they sit at the rug for meeting but is close to me.

In spite of my concerns, I want to support the work Lynn and Robert are doing with Katya's social worker. I decide to introduce the system for all the children, so that Katya is not singled out for separation from the group. I count "one" as the children laugh at her silly faces and "two" as she grabs my leg. She knows that I expect her to sit at meetings without interrupting by being silly. I put my arm around her gently. I always have Katya sit next to me so I can remind her that I'm paying attention to her, even when I'm talking to the whole class. But instead of relaxing, she burrows her head into my side until it hurts. The children laugh again.

"Three," I say. She knows she has to go to color. This transition takes a couple of minutes, and meanwhile I've lost the attention of the group and must start over.

Katya often makes me feel that I'm not a good teacher. Not only

---

1. Brenda McCreight, *Parenting Your Adopted Older Child* (Oakland, CA: New Harbinger, 2002).

do I fail, daily, to help her build more constructive relationships with her peers, but also her disruptions put me in danger of losing the focus of the group at any moment. She keeps her friends in a constant state of agitation as they vie for her attention, and if she and I are in competition for their interest, she wins hands down. The "time-ins" seem to help—she frequently needs only the first or second warning. When she does need to leave the group, she returns more settled—but her need to be the constant center of attention remains.

My own need to succeed in helping her puts me at a further disadvantage. I love to watch children develop new skills and am disappointed when I don't seem to be succeeding. Yet by allowing Katya to make me feel like a failure, I believe I give her too much power, just as the girls in her social group rely too much on her good favor.

Fortunately, there are other children in my class who give me a different message: I can see them grow and flourish under my care. It would be hard to be a parent of such a child without such a roomful of counterevidence.

As I have learned more about children like Katya who experienced early neglect and abuse, I have discovered that they often have difficulties in relationships with both adults and peers.

A newborn infant typically sleeps, wakes up, gets comforted and fed, and goes back to sleep. This cycle, over time, shows the child that his caregivers can be trusted, and eventually the child comes to believe the world around him will be predictable and will meet his needs.

A neglected infant, on the other hand, sleeps, wakes up, cries, goes back to sleep. He wakes, cries, goes back to sleep; wakes, cries, is fed, goes back to sleep. If he didn't get fed sometimes, he would die. But the inconsistency of care leads him to believe, over time, that the world cannot be trusted to meet his needs. As he gets older, he may come to rely on himself to an unusual degree. If he comes abruptly into a home with parents who want to love and care for him, he has no reason to believe they will be there for him in the future and no experience with trusting relationships. He may find their wish for intimacy disturbing, even frightening.

In addition to these environmental factors, the exposure to stress that most international adoptees are exposed to both pre- and post-natally may have long-lasting effects on attachment as well as on growth, the immune system, mental illness, and behavior.[2] Over time, if the child continues to fight desperately against this closeness, he may be diagnosed with reactive attachment disorder.

There are controversies about the treatment for this disorder, known as RAD. Some experts recommend an intensive and directive approach, using a series of sessions designed to show the child that the parent is both in control and caring. Other experts insist that time and consistent good care, including some of the bonding experiences typical of infancy, will eventually show the child that the adults can be trusted.

Many children who experienced early neglect have less extreme symptoms but still have difficulties with attachment. How could a child who has never known a consistent caregiver suddenly be able to love and be dependent on an adult? These children may, with time, develop closeness with their adoptive parents, but like Katya, they may continue to be manipulative, controlling, and demanding, or they may be clingy or have little impulse control.

Robert and Lynn do not know whether Katya was abandoned on the street in her carriage, but when they picked her up at the orphanage they saw that she was force-fed until she threw up, and then fed some more. Now, watching Katya as she tries always to be at the center of the group, I imagine her feeling that if she loses our attention, even for a moment, she could die of neglect. But when she has our focus, she does something to make us angry, perhaps frightened by the very closeness she seeks or unable to be satisfied by it.

It's as if she were trying to make her friends and the adults who care for her feel as she did in infancy—picked up and then abandoned, over and over. I have watched her daily, and I still don't understand how she keeps the constant attention of the other girls in the classroom, each one wanting to be her most special friend.

2. Miller, *Handbook of International Adoption Medicine*, 131.

I know she will reject the new chosen one, to start again with the next soon-to-be-disappointed favorite.

After the meeting is over, the children are on their way out to recess when I stop her. "Katya," I say, "I need to talk with you about the Mama business."

She looks puzzled but not opposed to a conversation about whatever it might be. She never holds my authority against me.

"I would be happy to pretend to be your mama," I say, "but not in a way that interrupts our meeting. So how could we do that?"

She gives me a quick smile. "Outside?" she says.

"Outside would be good. And then when we're at the rug sitting next to each other, what can you do so you can feel close without interrupting?"

"Just go close to you but not hold on?"

"That would be perfect," I say. "Can you do that without being silly?"

"Yes, like this." She leans comfortably against me.

This girl knows all the right answers. Now maybe I can be a good teacher. Maybe I can help Katya put together some strategies for dealing with her need for attention. Or maybe Katya will teach me to live with the idea that I don't have to solve her problems quickly: that my job is to keep trying, showing her that over time the adults in her new world won't desert her and can meet her needs, so that someday she'll believe this, too.

* * *

The next morning at meeting she won't stop making silly faces at Lily, who laughs and nudges Elisabeth. I count to three and send Katya off to color.

"Good-bye, Mama," she squeaks.

* 8 *

Gravity

On a square table I set out a special set of blocks and marbles for building ramps and tunnels. It includes long troughs that can be set at an incline as well as small cubes with marble-sized holes through the center for tunnels that can be set either vertically, to increase speed, or horizontally. Jasper and Keith begin to meet at this table first thing in the morning. Few words pass between the boys as they silently try to master physical concepts of inertia, gravity, and acceleration. Carefully, each lines up tunnels and troughs into a flat row and gives the marbles a push at the beginning and again near the end, where they drop into a small basin. The boys have not yet realized the excitement that will come when they add height at the beginning to increase the marbles' speed and make the initial push unnecessary.

They watch each other. Day by day their designs change, adding a little speed as they discover the effect of gravity on acceleration. They begin to laugh, often using nonsense words I do not understand. By adding more height, they discover that they can make the marbles go around a corner. A few days later they begin to converse. Two marble rolls are joined into one, necessitating the taking of turns. By making the starting point perilously high, they find they can get up enough speed to knock down several small plastic bears at the bottom, resulting in increased laughter.

But unlike Jasper, Keith has other friends. One morning Jasper is waiting for him at the marble roll table when he realizes that Keith is heading instead for the puppy house being built by Felipe and Shawn in the block area. Jasper's face starts to crumple; he goes to the cubby room and hides it in his hands.

"Why is Jasper crying?" Keith asks me.

"I think he expected you to play at the marble roll with him," I say. "But you don't have to do that. It's OK for you to choose something different if you want to."

"How about I'll play half the time in blocks and half in marble roll?"

"Why don't you ask him?" I suggest.

Keith goes into the cubby room and reappears with Jasper, who is smiling. Keith keeps his promise, playing first at the marble roll and then in the adjacent block area, while Jasper continues his experiments with gravity.

* 9 *

The Story of Robot Dog

"Then there was a dog," Jasper's story begins. "And the dog ate food. Then he saw the friend, Robot Dog. And they go to the park. And then they saw his friend Bird. And then he goes home to Bird's house. They eat lunch. The end."

* * *

Jasper's dog is making friends.

* 10 *

The Birthday Rule

"Katya said she'll only invite Caleb and Elisabeth to her birthday," Lily complains right before dismissal. "And she's copying us, and she said she would invite Ariel, too, and she said that she would play with us at recess, but she didn't!"

It's a long list, but not an unusual assortment of accusations against Katya, who is at the hub of the girls' social life. All the girls in the class want to sit by her and want to be her chosen friend, even though they must know, as I do, that she is likely to turn against them at any moment.

"Right," Caleb says. "Well, I had a idea for some . . . well this is a new rule about birthdays. Every time, nobody can't talk about birthdays unless . . . who all . . . they can invite . . . they have to invite everybody in the class."

"That's right!" I say, delighted that Caleb has applied the appropriate rule to the problem. "We've said that if you can't invite everyone for a birthday, you're not supposed to talk about it in school, so people don't feel sad, just the way Lily is right now."

"Well, I think it's really no fair if she only invites Caleb and the other people," Felipe agrees. "She didn't say Keith and like Shawn, or like she didn't say a lot of people." Felipe has power with the boys, and his opinion will hold weight.

"There's this other rule, too," Ariel adds, "that you can't talk about play dates. If you're having a play date, then just keep it in your head and not talk about it."

"Well, how about this is the rule," Ben says. "How about no talking about things that make people sad, like I can't play, and like we can't talk about things like where we're going, and things like that."

Ben rarely speaks at a class meeting, but his wish to be included in play is so strong that he is compelled to join in.

"I can't invite everybody to my birthday, 'cause I'm going to the Y to go rock climbing and there's not enough room," Katya says, speaking for the first time.

"So what could you do?" I ask her. "People are feeling quite upset about this."

"I could have a swimming party, and I could invite everybody," she says.

"So if you decide to have a swimming party and invite everyone, you can talk about it during school, but if you aren't inviting everyone, could you please stop talking about it in school? You're making some people very sad."

"OK, I forgot about that rule," she says.

Flexibility

At lunchtime, Katya opens her 101 Dalmatians lunchbox, looks inside, and complains loudly that there's nothing she likes. She is rarely happy with what she finds in her box, even though her parents try to give her food she likes and they take her to the grocery store so she can choose from a healthy selection of snack and lunch foods. After lunch, when she hasn't eaten, she becomes more unreasonable with her friends and with me. By dismissal time, she is often at her worst.

I consider asking her parents, Lynn and Robert, to come in for a conference. I don't know whether Katya's unhappiness at lunch is related to her early feeding experiences, but maybe together we can figure out what to do at school.

Jasper, too, has a hard time in the afternoons. He eats quietly, never complaining about his food. But after lunch he seems very tired, lying down when I read a book to the class after quiet time and sitting passively at the rug when it's time to put on his jacket, get his lunchbox, and get ready to go home.

Remembering that we had agreed to have a series of conversations during the school year, I decide to ask Lynn, Robert, and Gwen if they would be willing to continue our discussion, talking about issues around food and sleep.

"One of the things that I think worked out really well at Katya's preschool was everything nutritional there," Robert says, opening the discussion. "Especially for kids from Russia and Eastern European countries, underweight and under height, it was important that her preschool was the kind of place where food flowed freely, a lot of different kinds of food. The kids brought in their own food, but the staff had their own kitchen, and they would go to the ends of the earth to make sure that there was something appealing to the kids."

Robert explains that the teachers shared food with the kids and involved them in food preparation. "It is great for every kid to learn where the food comes from and how it's prepared. But I think that for adopted kids who need to have control over eating, like our child did and still does, that was probably pretty helpful."

Jasper preferred eating meat, from the time he was adopted at six months. "I think a lot of schools would not feed him that," Gwen tells us. "When the kids brought that kind of food in, the caregivers might say he's going to choke. We had an issue over apples, because at one point Jasper's sister Kalli, who's from a domestic adoption, was not eating well in her day care situation and we pulled her out, because I would send her in with whole apples and that was how she ate them. And they refused to give them to her and said that I would have to cut the apples up into little tiny bites with no peel. Her pediatrician wanted her to eat the peel, and she could; she was fine. And what they came back with was 'What if some other child grabs it out of her hand and takes a bite out of her apple? Then that child might choke.' And I said, 'Well, that's your job, you know.' And I would think for adopted children, that's a big issue. The day care has to be willing to provide the food the way your child will eat, be-cause often they won't eat anything when they first come here: new tastes, new temperatures, new whatever. Or they eat everything, including paint and paper. So the caregivers have to be very willing to experiment a little bit with what our nutritional guidelines are."

"We had issues with Katya with her naps," Lynn says. "When she would wake up she was a bear. And they had to develop a strat-egy when I was picking Katya up, because I have a bad back and I couldn't carry her if she was screaming and kicking. And I ex-plained, 'I don't know what's going on with Katya, if this is related to her orphanage issues or what, but she wakes up horribly,' and they got as creative as they could get with me to help get her home. They would have kids play around her while she was still sleeping so she would wake up to a kid kind of stepping on her mat, and then I would be sitting either outside the room or in the other end of the room, because if she woke up and saw me first, she'd start screaming. She had to wake up and be totally alert and start engaging in play before I would let her see me. I would never go to her; I would just wait for her to come to me, like a strange dog." Lynn is a veterinarian and tends to see people in animal terms. "Somebody would even walk her to the car with me. Sometimes one of her friends would come out at the same time with a parent and we would leave together."

At naptime, they would put her next to a child who slept longer, as Katya did. "Everybody else would be spread out perfectly evenly," Robert says, "so they wouldn't disturb each other while they were flailing around during their nap. But they would pair Katya up with somebody on mats on the floor; they would put the two mats right next to each other."

"Jasper had some night terrors, but not as regularly as another little girl in his preschool who came over from Cambodia," Gwen says. "She was a little older than he was; she was three when she came here. A lot of the kids that come from Cambodia have a hard time with cribs, because the babies are used to swinging baskets or hammocks. In the orphanage the older kids slept on mats on the floor. If they're put in a crib that doesn't move and has these bars, they have a hard time at home or in day care going to sleep, but if you put them on the floor they are fine. So it's another instance of paying attention to how they sleep and then seeing if you can help them with that."

I return to the question of Katya's lunch, wanting to be as flexible as the caregivers they have described so eagerly. "Do you think it would help Katya if we let her eat anytime she wanted instead of waiting for snack and lunch time?" I ask.

"We don't want you to treat her differently from the other children," Robert says. "I think that it's reasonable to expect kids this age to wait for a while to eat."

I think about Katya's need to control her life as much as possible. "Here's a wild idea," I say. "I don't know if it makes sense or not. What if you give her two lunchboxes so she can reject one right away and still have some food to eat?" We all laugh but agree it might be worth a try.

We think about Jasper's difficult afternoons. Even though he may have had only a few hours of sleep, he never naps during our quiet time. Maybe I just need to be more flexible; I could let him rest away from the rest of the group while I read the story, and I could give him more help getting ready to go home, rather than expecting him to do it himself.

We decide to try these changes and see what happens.

11

Teaching Him Stuff

Caleb is in the block area building motorcycles—one for Jasper and one for himself. Each seat is made from a block the size of a small shoebox that sits on top of a vertical block that is two feet high and six inches wide, forming a T that can swivel a little as the rider leans from side to side.

"Hold on tight, man," he tells Jasper. "This is gonna be a hard time." He looks up and sees I'm smiling. "I'm teaching him all this stuff," he tells me.

"Let me see if it's all screwed up," he tells Jasper. "Get off your motorcycle for a minute."

Jasper gets off and follows Caleb, who is walking around the blocks, inspecting them carefully. "You shouldn't drive," Caleb warns him. "Part of this screw came off. Here: BZZZZ." Caleb makes the sound of a power screwdriver. "This is for a big man. You want to go to motorcycle school?"

"Do I have to go like this, too?" Jasper asks, invisible screwdriver in his hand.

I'm sure that Caleb believes he's teaching Jasper about motorcycle maintenance, but as I see it, he's teaching Jasper how to pretend.

"Hop on," Caleb says as he puts his arm around Jasper, helping the younger boy up to sit behind him. "I'll give you all the space I can use." Jasper, who often corrects other children's grammar, does not seem to worry about Caleb's confused pronoun. "OK, we're there. Now you can go on yours." Jasper goes back to his own motorcycle and they ride for a while side by side, Caleb making the sound of his roaring engine.

"Actually," Caleb says, "you want to make a band? If you want to be an electric guitar man, you have to have one of these." He dismounts and hands Jasper a block about two feet long and four inches in diameter, takes one for himself, and shows Jasper how to hold it like an electric guitar, complete with swaggering hips. "This is how it goes: BOOM, BOOM, BOOM! I gotta get a chair. You know, electric guitar men gotta have chairs." He disassembles the motorcycles and transforms them into two seats. "You gotta sit here." But Jasper is a foot or so shorter than Caleb and he can't get up on his chair. Caleb takes out three of Jasper's blocks, replaces them with smaller ones, and then goes to sit on his own taller structure. "BOOM, BOOM, BOOM!" he demonstrates as Jasper plays, silently, beside him.

* 12 *

Land Mines

"To start our month-long nonfiction unit, you are invited to come in to the classroom to tell a brief story about your child," my note home says. I explain that parents can sign up to come in any morning to tell about a true incident, from the past or from the present, about the child.

Parents start coming in, one a day, to tell their stories, usually with the child whispering suggestions in the storyteller's ear. We discover that at Elisabeth's first baseball game she asked, "When is it over?" in the second inning but played happily with a large empty box of popcorn for the rest of the game. We find that Keith is learning a special kind of Japanese wrestling with his dad, and they demonstrate Keith's exceptional ability to climb up his father's leg and around his outstretched arms ten times without stopping or setting foot on the ground.

Early one morning, as I am on my way to the school kitchen to make my tea, I meet David, Jasper's dad, just after he has dropped Jasper off at our early morning program.

"Jasper wants me to tell a story about the time he learned to ride a two-wheeler," David tells me. "But he wants me to leave out the part where he fell off."

We laugh, imagining how short that story would be.

"But I've decided to tell the story of our trip to Cambodia to get him."

"Do you think he'll be OK with that?" I ask. David is not one to push his own agenda on Jasper, but I'm worried.

"When I told him I wanted to tell the story of his adoption, he didn't say, 'No, absolutely not, I don't want to talk about that.'"

"How did you decide it was time to do this?" I ask. "How did you know he's ready, even though it's not the story he wanted?"

"Last month, when you asked the children to make a web of pictures that told about important parts of their lives, we had set out a lot of different pictures and made suggestions," he says. "One of the things he chose was a map of Cambodia. But you mentioned that when he showed his web to the class, he just said, 'I like maps.' And he didn't talk about the fact that he was born in Cambodia. And to me, that implies that he was not proud of that bit of heritage. It's like he knows it, but he doesn't celebrate it. Gwen and I believe he should be celebrating it. He should be proud of it, and we want to model that behavior.

"So then I took out all of our photo albums, with his baby pictures and his adoption story, and I sat him down and I walked him through it and I talked to him about things. And he was excited. He was interested. He wanted to see the pictures of himself as a baby; he wanted to see the pictures of Cambodia. It's not that this was new, but it was beyond 'Oh, these are cute pictures of me as a baby.' It was more that he was interested in what the houses look like, where the airport and the orphanage were on the map; it had more of an intellectual impact rather than just the emotional one of 'these are my baby pictures.' And that was a clue to me that kids his age will probably find these things interesting, too."

* * *

I'm still nervous about Jasper's reaction a few days later when David comes in with him to tell his story. Instead of sitting on a small chair next to his dad, Jasper sits in the middle of the group of children, and at first I can't find him; his head is down and he's a bit hunched over. But that doesn't mean he is upset. Eye contact is not comfortable for him, and he may want to avoid having to look directly at his friends while his dad talks about him.

"This is the story of how my son Jasper came to America and found his forever family," David begins. "We first learned about Jasper when he was three months old, and all that we knew was that he was living in a small orphanage in Cambodia just outside of Phnom Penh. We didn't know anything else about where he was born or who his parents were. We just knew that he was a three-month-old little boy who was pretty healthy and needed a family. And Cambodia is almost exactly on the exact opposite side of the earth from where we live in Massachusetts. If you were to take a globe and place a pencil through Massachusetts and straight through the center of the globe, it would come out the other end almost exactly in Cambodia. So when the time finally came to go and find Jasper, he was six months old by then. We had to get on a very big airplane and fly halfway around the world to a very big airport in Singapore, and then get on a medium-sized airplane to fly to a medium-sized airport in Vietnam, and then get on a little airplane to fly to a little airport in Phnom Penh. And the trip took thirty hours, almost a day and a half of travel time, to go all the way around the world to find this little boy. And even when we were traveling we still didn't know very much about him. We had seen a few pictures of him, but we didn't know much except that he was a beautiful little brown-skinned, black-haired boy with a kind of bewildered expression on his face.

"When we arrived in Cambodia we were tired and very travel-worn, both of us feeling like we needed a shower, but they whisked us right from the airport to the orphanage, and within half an hour we had this little boy placed in our arms, and he wasn't scared, wasn't worried, smiled at us, cooed and giggled for us. We asked about what he would like to eat, and the woman who took care of him, a beautiful woman named Kunthea who was his nanny in Cambodia, told us that he was eating just about everything—bread and fish and pork. They didn't have very much formula because it's an expensive thing for them to buy in Cambodia. So he was drinking cow's milk and goat's milk and pretty much eating everything that they were eating. And we were kind of amazed at this; at six months he was on solid food and everything else. But when we got him to the hotel where we were staying, sure enough, we sat down to dinner and he grabbed some bread and immediately started chewing on it and started eating noodles. He was hungry because at the orphanage they didn't have a lot of food. And to this day he still loves to eat—he loves noodles, it's his favorite thing ever. Spaghetti is his favorite food.

"And from that very young age he was always outgoing, always loved to look at people. Very quiet, never got upset, never cried. Very brave little boy. And we got on the little plane to go back to Massachusetts and flew in the little plane to the medium-sized airport and then in the medium-sized airplane to go to the big airport and then finally onto the big airplane for the thirty-hour trip back to Massachusetts. He quite happily rode in the plane the whole time, and to this day he still likes to ride on big rides. He loves the roller coaster, and he's not afraid of the Ferris wheel, and he's just a kid who loves to ride in big vehicles. So little things from his babyhood have carried over to his little childhood. So that's my story of Jasper."

"Why didn't they have a lot of food?" Felipe asks as soon as David has finished his story. Felipe goes to Brazil to visit his extended family every summer. Maybe he has a clearer image of a place where food can sometimes be scarce.

David hesitates. "Well, there were wars in Cambodia, and a lot of the land that could be used for farming can't be used."

"Why not?" Felipe pursues the problem.

A longer pause. "The soldiers left land mines on the fields, and it's not safe to walk there."

My heart sinks. I know it will be a long time before we get back to Jasper's adoption.

"What happens if you walk there?"

"Does it explode?"

"What if you stand on top of it?"

There is an outburst of excitement at the idea. I step in to protect David and Jasper.

"Jasper's dad is here to talk about Jasper's story. We'll talk about land mines and war later," I add, knowing I will have to force myself to follow up on this. "But I want you to know that there are no land mines here. Cambodia is as far away from us as you can get."

"Whew!" Felipe says. "That was lucky!"

* * *

I listen to their play all day, waiting to hear if anyone is playing Cambodian land mines. But all I hear is one adoption game.

"Pretend we're adopted and we're living on the street."

"Pretend I'm the mom. I come by and ask if you want to be adopted."

"I'd love to be adopted."

Elisabeth looks up and sees I'm listening.

"That reminds me of the story Jasper's dad told today," I say.

"But he was *really* adopted," she says. "Did he have a mom before he was adopted?"

"Yes, he did. He had a mommy and a daddy, and they couldn't take care of him, and so he had to go to the orphanage so he would have somebody who would love him and take care of him until he could get a new mommy and daddy."

"Why?"

"I think his mommy was very, very sick and wasn't able to take care of him," I say. "I can ask David about that."

"Oh," she answers, satisfied, and turns back to her game.

The next morning I look for David before school and ask him how he felt about telling the story.

He laughs. "When I went home I told Gwen, 'Well, I think I was doing OK until I tripped over a land mine.' She said, 'We're going to get one of those group e-mails from Jane: "Dear parents, if your child's asking about land mines and bombs . . ."'"

"I listened to their play," I say, "but I didn't hear anything except some children playing a game about being adopted. I wanted to ask you about the way I handled it."

I recap Elisabeth's question and my answer.

"I told her that I thought Jasper's mom was too sick to take care of him. Was there a different answer that you would prefer?" I realize, as I say this, that prior to my discussions with the parents of adopted children I might not have thought to ask this question.

"I think the answer that Gwen and I have come to is that Jasper did have a mom and his mom knew that she couldn't take care of him the way she wanted him to be taken care of, and so she went and found somebody who could take care of him. So that way, it leaves open whether or not she's sick or whether she's poor or whether it's that her house is not good. It's that she loved him so much she wanted to find a better place for him to be."

I ask if it is OK for me to tell this to the other children. With most children, I would tell them to ask the child involved. But I know that would make Jasper so uncomfortable that he would be unlikely to be able to answer.

"Yes," David agrees. "That's fine. It's a total fiction—we don't know much about his birth mother, and with some of the revelations about Cambodian adoption that have come out in the last couple of years, he could have been bought from his birth mother. This story is a comfortable fiction, but it's broad enough to encompass all possible facts."

"When you told the story to the kids, I noticed that you spent about half the time on transportation," I say. "I'm sure that Jasper appreciated that. How did you decide what to say in your story and what not to say?"

"That's something that kids can relate to," David says. "Kids can relate to traveling in the car, how it's long and boring. I'm not a very good storyteller; Gwen's a much better storyteller than I am."

"The kids were spellbound," I tell him. I've been noticing that all the parents are more nervous about their stories than I had expected they would be.

"But I feel like repetition and having something that sort of frames a story helps," he says, "so you can start off with an idea that is the beginning of the story, getting on the airplane, and then come back to it at the end of the story. It gives them a starting point and an end point that is recognizable, so that when you get to the end of the story they understand this is how the story ends; we heard that in the beginning. It also helps me pace out my thoughts, by starting off with the big airplane to the big airport to the littler airplane to the littler airport; that kind of thing helps me think about this in small steps. Because when I talk to adults about it, I jump right to the meat of the story. The kids are not going to be interested or have any way of relating to the overwhelming emotional impact of being in a foreign culture, meeting this little tiny person that you've been waiting for four months to finally get a chance to see and hold and touch and smell, and that's something that they're just not going to relate to. And maybe it's not appropriate for them to be trying to think about those things. That's my story—it's not Jasper's story.

That's the only thing that I didn't like about what I had done; it was supposed to be a story about Jasper, and it was really more of a story about Gwen and me than it was about Jasper."

I've always thought of David as a bit shy, someone who might be uncomfortable telling stories to a group of kids. I know he has not done this before. But this story is important to him, and he's made excellent decisions about how to tell it.

"So when I sat down to talk about this," he continues, "I felt like this is something that's important about his heritage because it makes him unique from all of his classmates, but it also kind of highlights things that are the same: he likes noodles, he likes to ride on airplanes, and he likes roller coasters. I wanted to talk about why where he comes from makes him special and why where he comes from may influence the things that he likes and doesn't like today. And honestly, I think it's one of the most interesting things about him. The story about riding his bike really was not that much of a grabber of a story."

"Especially if you leave out the falling-down part," I say. "But then you hit a land mine. How did you decide how to answer their questions about war?"

"Well, it started when I said that they didn't have a lot of food. And somebody asked why it was they didn't have a lot of food, and I said, 'Well, it was a war-torn country, and a lot of the land that would be used for farming was not useful because of land mines.'"

"And then you stopped right there. And then someone asked why they couldn't grow anything on that land."

"If Jasper had asked me those questions, I'd be very, very frank. I would really lay out the ugly truths about our country's first involvement in Cambodia and Cambodian history and everything else."

"Has he ever asked?" I say.

"No, he has not ever asked. I figure once he's ready to ask, he's ready to know. But I also felt really uncomfortable putting that into other people's children, because my perspective on honesty and what kids are prepared to handle isn't shared by every parent."

"And one kid might be prepared to handle it but others might not," I add.

"I think that's the kind of conversation that is better held one on one," he agrees. "Because in the group there are going to be kids who are freaked out by it or who have questions that they're afraid to ask. And you traumatize them without being aware that you're doing it. So that's really tough."

"So how did you decide what to say and what not to say?" I ask. "I know you didn't have time to think it through at the time, but how do you see it now, looking back on it?"

"Well, you kind of rescued me, because you redirected the conversation back to Jasper, which helped a lot. Basically I took my cue from my work as a veterinarian, when I have to tell families that their animal is very ill or very injured and is not going to make it. I've had to have this conversation with small children fairly frequently."

Although I knew both Lynn and David were veterinarians, it had not occurred to me that a regular part of the job includes telling a young child that a pet is going to die.

"So the way I present it in my job is that there are things you can't change and you can't fix in this world, and this is one of those things. It's an ugly thing that can happen. Their pet is hurt very, very badly; it's in a lot of pain, and so I try to be compassionate but at the same time really matter-of-fact about it—yes, this is an awful thing but it's a fact of life. This seems to work well with kids. They realize that you're telling them that it's not fair and that's the way it is. They pick up on that pretty quickly. So that's basically the only thing that I had to draw on."

David is not an expert in child development, and yet by watching kids in his work and thinking about his own children, he has gained tremendous understanding of how to talk with them about important and difficult issues. I wonder whether all parents who have internationally adopted children have had to face these issues early, as they have thought through how, what, and when to tell their children about their adoption and their early life. If so, it's another reason to bring them into the classroom, where we can all learn from them.

Bringing Adoption into the Classroom

"When I invited parents to come in to tell stories about the children, I wasn't thinking about your adoption stories," I tell Robert, Lynn, and Gwen during our next conversation. "So I'd like to go back to an issue we talked about in our first discussion: how much do you want to bring adoption issues into the classroom, and what can the teacher do to help make the transition smoother?"

"I think teachers need to be flexible with parents, just like they need to be flexible with the kids," Robert says. "There are parents for whom assimilation is a priority, and there are others who want their child to have distinct recognition as being adopted."

"Well for me," Lynn says, "Katya was going through the clingy, clingy thing where she wouldn't let go and I was like, 'She's going to drive this teacher nuts.' I just wanted to talk to you to let you know that she's got some insecurities. One of them is that she has to hold and hold and hold and doesn't let go. She did it with kids, and some kids really didn't like it. And we all talked about how that was a neediness insecurity thing related to the adoption. I was so worried that she wasn't going to have any friends. I just wanted you to understand so that you could facilitate the whole thing in the classroom."

Gwen says, "I think we come from opposite places. You wanted the teacher to know your child was adopted so that she would be aware of behavior problems and would attribute those problems potentially to the adoption. She would think about new ways to address them, and not judge you as the bad parent because your child had them but would collaborate with you. For me, I wanted my teacher to be aware of the adoption but not see it as impacting Jasper in his behaviors—to see his behaviors as independent of the adoption. There was that sense of that 'My child's exceptional be-cause my child comes from a different place, but don't you tell me my child's *different* because he comes from a different place. You know, I can criticize but you can't.'"

"What would you like a teacher to know at that first confer-ence?" I ask.

"At that first conference, I think I would have wanted you to say something more to the point of 'So Jasper's adopted from Cambo-dia; how old was he when he was adopted? Oh, he was six months old. Is there anything that you think he carries with him from his adoption? I know that sometimes children have some social issues, or sleeping issues, or food issues or any number of things. Do you think he carries anything with him?'"

"Instead of making an assumption," I say.

"Right," she agrees. "And I would have then said, 'No, I don't think so.' You might have then said, 'I don't know, but I see this and this.' And that would have opened a conversation."

Robert goes into the kitchen and returns with a plate full of fruits and vegetables. Our crunching of carrots gives me a chance to for-mulate my response.

"So the first thing you want in your child's school or day care," I say when we return to the conversation, "is a teacher who is willing to listen to you without passing judgment—someone who will work with you if problems come up. What else do you look for?"

"I never wanted Jasper to be a special kid," Gwen says. "Even when I thought I was giving birth to children, I said, 'I just want av-erage kids. I don't want them to be exceptional in any way. Just give me the middle kid.' But at the same time, I am extremely proud of the fact that my family was built through adoption. It's a big piece of my identity, and I take every opportunity I can to tell people."

"You're trained to tell your children their stories over and over again so they feel comfortable with them," Lynn says. "At night we still talk about Katya's story."

"We have a book of photos about our trip to Cambodia to get Jasper," Gwen says. "It sits on his bedside table."

"And you want that to be such a comfortable thing for them. It would feel funny if it got glossed over in school," Lynn says. "Katya might feel like 'what's so special at home is a big part of me—don't sweep it under the rug at school because I'm not supposed to be proud of it outside of the house.'"

I ask how they would want that to be addressed at school.

"I was really proud of having built our family through adoption," Robert says. "So when I went into the preschool, I told the people in the day care classroom, and I told other parents that I met."

"Most adoptive parents are like that, I think," Gwen says. "That's a big piece of you."

"That was not true when I started teaching," I say. "Parents often didn't tell me at the first conference. Sometimes it came out later, as though they were telling me a secret. I remember one family that had not even told the child."

"At that time they would have been told, 'Don't talk about it. Pretend you don't notice it, close your eyes,'" Gwen says. "And now people are saying to talk about it because we're proud of it. We want our kids to be proud of it and we want their friends to be proud of it."

Lynn adds, "When we meet people in their forties or fifties who are adopted and we talk about our kids, they say, 'I think this is so great; when I was a kid no one talked about adoption.'"

"But how do we pull it back into the classroom?" Gwen asks. "How openly do you talk about it in school? I think as a parent I want it open. I think there should be *Koala for Katie* and all these little books on adoption for preschoolers sitting on the shelf along with Dr. Seuss."

"Maybe your adoption day should be celebrated with your classmates," Lynn says.

"I think that's a question for a teacher to bring up to a parent as well," Gwen says. "When you find out their child's adopted, the question is 'How much or how little would you like me to try to bring adoption or Cambodia or Russia into what we do in our classroom?'"

"And maybe you should ask, 'How would your child feel about that in the classroom?'" Lynn says.

"I would ask Katya," Robert says. "Katya's old enough for me to say, 'Would it embarrass you?' No," he corrects himself, "I might say, 'Would you like it if they talked about adoption in your class? How would that make you feel?'"

I note that in his first phrasing of the question—"Would it embarrass you"—Robert realized he could be suggesting to Katya that the subject might be embarrassing, while his revision, the more open phrasing "Would you like it if they talked about adoption," implies that talking about adoption openly in school would be fine. I find it reassuring that we can all keep working on these issues, not expecting to be perfect.

"It comes up spontaneously, too," I say. "I heard that one day you walked in to pick Jasper up from the after-school program, Gwen, and Jasper said, 'Hi, Mom,' and then one of the older kids said, 'That's Jasper's mom?' and then looked at Jasper and said, 'Are you adopted?'"

"Jasper was fine with it," Gwen says. "He said, 'Yeah.'"

"I heard about the incident," I say, "from an adult in the after-school program who wondered if he should step in and say something. He wanted to help Jasper, in case he was uncomfortable, but he didn't know the best way to do it. That's an issue that teachers and other people who work at the school need to talk about, too."

I'm beginning to understand how parents may want their children to be regular kids but at the same time they may need to ask for accommodations to be made; how they want to be acknowledged for the way they have built their families through adoption but they may be worried about the reactions of others. These three parents have thought carefully about what their children may need in order to thrive and feel safe, and they looked for preschools that would be flexible enough to meet those needs.

I tell them about a mother who let me know that her daughter, adopted from Russia, needed to rock back and forth in order to soothe herself, as many children do who have not had enough early stimulation. Her kindergarten teacher would not allow her to rock in school, even though the child was quiet and not disruptive. Her mother was distraught—it did not seem possible to stop her child's rocking, and she did not know what to do.

Gwen, in contrast, is ready to change schools when she believes the caregivers are not flexible enough to meet her child's nutritional needs. All three of these parents are willing to look without flinching at their children's needs and find caregivers who meet those needs, even when they are out of the ordinary.

"I have an idea of another way to bring adoption into the classroom," Gwen says. "I'd like to come in to tell a story, too. But it's fiction," she warns me. "I wrote it about Jasper's name when he was in preschool."

I tell her that's fine. We'll use it to talk about the difference between fiction and nonfiction.

* 13 *

Far Away from the Tigers

A few days later, Gwen is sitting on the big chair in the front of the room. Jasper is in the front row of children sitting at her feet.

In a faraway land where the winds blew hot and the land was dry, a young woman lay very still on a sleeping mat on the floor of her dusty cottage. In her arms lay a tiny boy, no more than a few weeks old.

The woman was very, very tired, and very, very sick. She had nearly collapsed just a few days before, when a wild tiger chased her down the hot, sandy paths of the village. But love had made her strong. She hugged her baby boy tightly and ran faster than the wind, finding safety in her small cottage in the leafy jungle.

"You are so brave," she told her son. "When the tiger growled and snapped at our heels, you never cried. I was so tired, I thought I would trip and fall. But when I looked in your eyes, I found strength and courage." The little boy smiled up at the young woman and made happy baby sounds.

The woman continued, "Little One, you must continue to be brave. This place is filled with great danger, and I am too sick to keep you safe. You need a mommy and a daddy who can feed you when you are hungry, give you water when you are thirsty, hug you when you are sad, and give you a comfortable place to rest where no tigers or other wild animals will threaten your safety. I cannot give you any of those things. So tomorrow I will take you to a special place where you will be safe until your mommy and daddy come for you. It will be scary to go to a new place where you will be surrounded by strangers. But you must be brave, and remember that I love you." The baby boy smiled at his birthmother as if to say that he understood. Then he cooed and fell asleep.

The next morning, the young woman wrapped the little boy in the only blanket she had, an old piece of carpet, tattered and torn. She wrapped him up tightly to keep the sun from burning his skin and the sand from stinging his eyes. Then she carried him to a special place—far, far away from the tigers.

The young woman kissed the little boy and placed him on the doorstep of an orphanage where kind women cared for little children. She knocked on the door and then quickly ran away.

A beautiful and gentle woman named Nally heard the knock and opened the door. At first she thought maybe the wind had rattled her old wooden door, as no one appeared to be outside. She looked to the right and she looked to the left . . . Then she looked down and saw the tiny bundle that lay at her feet. "Oh, my goodness!" she cried. "It's a little baby!"

Nally took the baby inside and began to open the blanket. "It's OK, baby," she whispered. "Don't be scared. Don't cry." But when she opened the blanket all the way, the little boy surprised her. He looked up at Nally with big brown eyes, and instead of crying, he smiled and laughed. "My goodness!" said Nally. "You must be a very brave little boy! You have had quite an adventure today, and still you are smiling. I'm going to call you Vireak [vi-wreck'], because that means BRAVE!"

During the next several months, Vireak lived very happily with Nally and her other children. He had food when he was hungry and water when he was thirsty, hugs when he was sad, and a soft bed to rest on when he was tired. Sometimes the wind would howl through the walls of the orphanage, and the little children would cry out. But not Vireak. Vireak would just listen to the wind and imagine that it was singing him a soft lullaby. "Vireak," the other children would say, "you are so brave."

One day Nally came to sit by little Vireak's feet. She had a special surprise, she told him. She had searched all over the world, and she had found the most wonderful mommy and daddy to adopt him.

"They will take you far, far away from the tigers, the stinging sands, the howling winds, and the hot, hot sun. They will give you food when you are hungry and water when you are thirsty, hugs when you are sad, and a soft bed to rest on when you are tired. But most important, they will give you love, forever and ever and ever. This mommy and daddy

want to be your forever family." Vireak gave Nally a little hug and looked at her with his big brown eyes. "It will be a little scary, Vireak," said Nally. "At first you will not know this mommy and daddy. And they will take you to a place that is much different from the jungle you know. But you must be brave, and remember that I love you." Vireak yawned and smiled.

The next day, a mommy and a daddy arrived in the jungle. They had traveled a long, long time in an airplane to find this special little boy. And now they were riding in the back of a taxi, through dense, leafy trees, where tigers peeked around every rock and root. They held hands tightly.

"What if he doesn't like me?" worried the mommy.

"He will," said the daddy. Then he hugged the mommy close.

"What if Nally changes her mind?" worried the mommy.

"She won't," said the daddy. And he gave her a gentle kiss in the middle of her forehead.

"I'm scared," said the mommy.

"Me too," said the daddy.

And suddenly they were parked in front of the door of the orphanage.

The mommy and the daddy knocked on the door and were greeted by the most beautiful sight they had ever seen: little Vireak, cuddled in Nally's arms, smiling up at them with his big brown eyes. "Be brave," Nally whispered in his ear. Vireak took one long look at Nally and then reached out to his new mommy.

"He's not afraid!" said the mommy.

"Not Vireak," said Nally. "Vireak is special. Vireak has courage."

The mommy and the daddy loved Vireak very much. They hugged him and kissed him and told him how lucky they felt to be chosen as his special forever family. And Vireak loved them back.

Everything seemed perfect. Well, almost perfect . . .

Vireak's new mommy and daddy lived in the United States, a place far, far away from the jungle. And they knew that people in the United States would have a hard time saying "Vireak." Some people said, "Vir-eeek" and others said "Vi-rack." It was very confusing. So Vireak's mommy and daddy decided to give their little boy a new name that everyone in the United States could say perfectly. They thought and thought. Daddy suggested Sage or Haven. Mommy suggested Jace or Jackson or Jeremiah. But none of these names seemed to fit just right.

Then one night, as they sat gazing at the starry sky, thinking about how lucky they were to have been given such a brave little boy to love as their very own, the mommy looked at the daddy and said, "I've got it! Let's name him Jasper, which means 'bringer of treasure.'" The daddy looked down at the little boy he held gently in his arms, and he whispered, "Yes. He will be Jasper Vireak. Our brave little boy. Our greatest treasure."

And that's how Jasper Vireak got his name.

"That's definitely not a true story," Katya says. "But I like it."

* 14 *

One Telephone Overboard

"That block goes over there," Glen tells Jasper early one morning.

Jasper needs both hands to pick up the hollow wooden block the size of a shoebox. He places it on the structure, now a wall surrounding the block area, which might become a house, a boat, or a puppy kennel before it's finished, and will be large enough for four children to play in. But Glen is not satisfied. "Not quite," he says. "Over there. Now we need one more."

Jasper picks up a square block and sets it on the corner of the building. "Not the square! Duh!" Glen says, laughing, and then Jasper laughs, too. Some children would take offense if another child laughed at what they'd done. Others would become clowns, pretending they had done it on purpose, to be silly. I'm not sure Jasper knows that Glen is laughing at his supposed mistake in choosing the square block. Or is he hiding his embarrassment by laughing with Glen?

Jasper and Glen are usually the first to arrive at school, where they attend our early-morning program. Recently I have begun to invite them to play in the classroom for that half-hour before the other children start to arrive. Glen loves being the first one to enter the block area in the morning, setting the stage for the games of the day. But my reason for encouraging this arrangement is to ensure Jasper a half-hour each day in the block area with just one other child. I am hoping that perhaps one day the pull of the game will be so strong that he will overcome his aversion to the noise and complexity of the group social interactions and forget to withdraw to his alphabet and his lists once the other boys arrive.

There are children who do not want to join the group—they

spend their days at the art table making increasingly complex projects, becoming comfortable sharing materials and ideas, and gradually forming friendships with the children around them. But Jasper, I am coming to believe, wants to join the group, and my goal is to help that to happen when he is ready.

I have been wondering why he feels so threatened by the increase in social interaction. I try to imagine what it is like to process language slowly, as he does. When someone asks him a question, he pauses a long time before putting his response into words. If he feels rushed, he won't answer at all.

I have the opposite problem: I tend to answer quickly and later wish I had taken more time to listen and to formulate my response. But I did have an experience that reminds me of Jasper. A few years ago, my family went to Costa Rica for a month to learn Spanish. Week by week, I saw my husband and daughter gain fluency while I struggled with basic vocabulary and grammar, making little progress. When asked a question, I had to process the sentence word by word, searching for vocabulary I could recognize. If I wanted to answer, I had to try to remember each word and verb form. If the listener was patient and did not make me feel too dumb, I might manage to get my meaning across. But if a conversation included several fast speakers I would quickly give up, letting the sound wash over me, knowing it would be hopeless to try to understand.

Perhaps this, then, is Jasper's experience in a crowded, noisy block area where there is constant quick negotiation of characters and plots.

For several mornings, he has been Glen's willing student in this art of play, copying his actions and words carefully, practicing the skills needed to build a setting, add characters, and develop a plot.

Now Jasper puts the square back on the shelf and takes out a rectangle, putting it on top of the building.

"There!" Glen finally approves. "That will hold it! Why don't you make another house? This is gonna be our bridge over here." He picks up a small rectangle and sets it vertically on the top. "This can be our thermometer, so we know what the temperchure is outside."

"It's gonna be thermometer!" Jasper agrees. "It's gonna be the temper . . . tem . . . cha . . . ture." I suspect Jasper could pronounce the word perfectly but is trying to copy Glen's more babyish pronunciation.

"The temperchure!" Glen corrects him, laughing.

"The block action!" Jasper says, laughing, too.

"What did you say?" I ask. I am not sure I heard him correctly. I wonder whether he's being silly to cover his embarrassment or whether he's changing the subject. Jasper does not like being corrected: he prefers to do everything perfectly the first time.

"Uh," he says, not answering my interruption.

"We don't need these blocks," Glen says, removing two that Jasper had placed earlier.

Jasper picks up a flat board that's six inches wide and a little longer than he is tall, and puts it across the top of the building for a roof. "Maybe we could put this over there," he says tentatively.

"Jasper," Glen says quietly, "that's not very good. So let's put it . . . outside." He moves the board to the floor outside the block enclosure. "This will go here—number one surfboard. Now we need one more surfboard," he says, putting a second board next to the first.

"Let's get out of here!" Jasper says, laughing as he moves out of the building to stand on surfboard number one.

"No, no, no, no, no! Don't! *Jas*-per." Glen lengthens Jasper's name as he criticizes his ideas. "Don't get out of there!" Glen points to a corner inside the structure. "Maybe this could be your bed, right here," he says, offering an incentive for Jasper to stay inside, where he wants him.

Jasper obediently comes inside and lies down, almost hidden behind the large blocks. "Jas-per! Jas-per!" Glen calls. Jasper does not answer. "Earth to Jasper! Are you home?"

I would not blame Jasper for being out of town. I am beginning to worry about the wisdom of the arrangement I have made for the boys to play together. I know Glen tends to pout when he doesn't get his way, but I did not expect him to reject every attempt Jasper made at autonomy.

Unable to stand his bossiness, I enter the scene for a second time.

"Jasper! Are you home?" I ask cheerfully, counteracting what I see as the latest putdown.

"No," Jasper answers.

"He's not home," I tell Glen. "You could leave a message on his answering machine."

"He's not here because he's at school," Glen says.

"No, I'm not at home yet. No, I'm not at school," Jasper says, disagreeing for the first time.

"Maybe you need telephones," I suggest, handing Glen two play phones from the dramatic play area, trying once more to do something to distract Glen from his apparent plan to put down any idea Jasper suggests.

So often I find myself aware of the tension between wanting to protect a child from experiencing pain and knowing that the child must learn to master his own challenges. I first became intensely aware of this tension the week my first child was born. I had assumed that I would be a good mother and thus I would have a happy baby. But every time my baby nursed, she cried. We walked her, burped her, rocked her, swaddled her. Nothing helped her upset stomach—each time she ate, she cried until she went to sleep. Helpless to soothe her, I realized that I would not be able to keep her from experiencing pain: all I could do was to be with her so she was not alone.

Ever since that day, I have had to learn over and over that not only is it impossible to take away another person's pain, but it is also not always the most valuable thing for me to do. What I really want for my daughter is resilience—for her to meet her own challenges and rebound from the disappointments that will surely occur as she tries to fulfill her own dreams. I hope she will also find support by sharing her dreams and disappointments with those she loves.

Still, my first impulse is to protect a child who might be hurt. Over and over, I have to remind myself to stand back and watch to see whether my help is really needed. Glen and Jasper are giving me one more opportunity to learn this lesson.

"Thank you! Telephones!" Glen says. "Hello, Jasper. What are you doing? Blah, blah, blah, blah, OK? I just canceled your message. Jasper! Get in your house!"

"I'm not here!" Jasper says. He realizes that if he's not here, he must not say so, and so he corrects his pronoun: "He's not here."

"Jasper!" Glen says, "I said, 'Get in your house!' Do you want to get punished?"

Realizing that my telephone intervention has been less than successful, I decide to restrain myself from interrupting again. Jasper is going to have to learn to deal with bossy players in his own way.

Jasper's telephone falls off the block where he's set it down. Perhaps it was off balance, or maybe he decided to push it, but he neatly slips the event into the plot. "No, wait!" he says. "My telephone went overboard! Nobody knows where we are!"

"I know that," Glen agrees without admitting that Jasper has had a good idea.

By ignoring Glen's demand and coming up with a new direction that is too exciting to resist, Jasper has changed the tone and the course of the game. But at this critical moment the other children enter the room and Jasper withdraws to the writing table, where he begins making a list of the months of the year in careful, tiny print.

∗ 15 ∗

One Baby Penguin

"Once upon a time there were two baby kittens who were born in a cardboard box behind the Hampton General Store," I say as the children settle down for snack at the rug. "They were brown and orange with white noses, and they looked just alike except that one had long hair and one had short hair."

Whenever I begin with "Once upon a time," the children are immediately silent and attentive. Storytelling is not something that comes easily to me, but today I have a reason to push my abilities: I am trying to find a way to encourage Katya's friends to stand up to her bossiness while at the same time letting Katya know that I respect her. And I don't have to invent a conflict for my story: I can take it directly from this morning's dramatic play.

"When they were hungry, the kittens ate the cheese stuck to the used pizza boxes that were stacked next to the garbage cans in back of the store. Their best friend was the chocolate-colored Lab puppy who lived in the big white house next door. He didn't eat from the garbage—he ate dog kibble, and if he begged, he got scraps from his owners' plates at dinner. When he got tired of staying in his yard, he dug a tunnel under the white picket fence and went to play with the kittens at the General Store. Their favorite game was Baby Bunnies. They pretended to be three baby bunnies who liked to play in the woods. Usually one of them got a foot caught in a trap, or they all got sick and had to go to the hospital.

"But one day, when the Chocolate Lab came to play, he was not in a good mood. The kittens said, 'Let's pretend the bunnies saw a hunter.' The Chocolate Lab said, 'I want to be the only baby bunny.'

"The kittens were shocked. They were used to the Chocolate Lab being a bit bossy, but this was different. 'But we want to be three baby bunnies, just like always!' they said.

"'Then I'll play One Baby Bunny all by myself,' the Chocolate Lab said. But the kittens didn't want to play Two Baby Bunnies without him. The Chocolate Lab always had the best ideas to make their games exciting."

"That upset the kitties," Elisabeth interrupts my story.

"That's like me and Lily and Katya," Ariel says. "Katya wants to play One Baby Penguin, but me and Lily want to play Three Baby Penguins."

"Katya could play something that boys play that don't like to be baby penguins, so Katya could be the only baby penguin in that game," Elisabeth says.

"We would be mad because we wanted to play with Katya, too," Ariel says.

"Katya's not really being fair," Keith says. "They should be whoever they want."

"I wanted to play alone," Katya says, scowling. "That's the whole point."

But I agree with Keith and silently cheer the girls on. Katya will stop manipulating their games and excluding them one by one only when they learn to support each other and stand up against her.

"Katya could be the only baby penguin, but then Lily and Ariel could be younger or older kids," Shawn says.

"No!" Ariel and Lily say. "That's not the way the game goes!"

"I meant just a little bit younger," Shawn says.

"What should the kittens do about the Chocolate Lab?" I say, returning to fiction since there seems to be a deadlock in our real-life negotiations.

"The kittens could say, 'You can be the only baby bunny today and we'll be the only baby bunny the next day,'" Glen says.

"Why does the puppy want to be the only baby bunny?" Lily asks.

I ponder Lily's interesting question. Would I have wanted to be the only baby bunny? I think I would have relished the security of the bunny family, always playing the game together. "Maybe it's because she has three brother and three sister puppies at home and she never gets to be the only one," I say, hoping to show Katya that I am not really down on the Lab puppy. He has an important point of view, too. But by jumping in, I lose the opportunity to hear what the children would say about it.

"I think they should say 'Eenie meeney miney moe,'" Ariel says. "And whichever gets 'moe' is the baby bunny."

"If they can't figure it out, Katya and Lily and Ariel can play the game with toys," Elisabeth says, going back to our original conflict.

"I think what Elisabeth meant was to play with the glass animals your mother gave us," Keith says. The children treasure the small china figures my mother collects from her Red Rose tea, and they often use them in their games. There are enough little figures to allow each child to "be" several animals in the game at one time, which can make the question of ownership of characters less intense.

I notice that it's time for recess and want to wrap up the discussion.

"Ariel and Lily," I say, "it does seem as though people agree with you that if you want to be baby penguins, you should find a way to do that."

"I'm agreeing, too," says Katya. "We'll all be the same size."

"We'll all be in our mama's stomach!" Ariel says, excited that Katya has agreed.

When I announce that it's time to get their jackets on, Ariel and Lily give Katya a quick triumphant glance and skip off holding hands.

Katya comes up to me and puts her head on my lap. "My tummy hurts," she says.

"That was hard," I tell her. "You had to listen to people who disagree with you. You heard what they said and you changed your opinion. Good job."

She burrows her head into my lap. "I want my mama," she says.

* 16 *

Exploded

Jasper is the best reader in the class; he can decode almost any word that he can understand. But there is a piece of the comprehension puzzle that he is missing—when he reads a book to me, he can understand a very simple, repetitive story, but if he reads anything more complex, when he comes to a word that he's not sure of, he substitutes gibberish. If there are several difficult words, he'll begin to mumble, making up words and even sentences, continuing as though he doesn't notice that he's making no sense.

Borrowing and reworking an idea from Sylvia Ashton-Warner, a New Zealand educator of the 1950s, I decide to make a list on the board of the children's most important words. For different reasons, I want both Jasper, an expert decoder, and Caleb, a nonreader who does not recognize most letters of the alphabet, to see that printed words can carry important meanings. I put each child's name on a three-by-five card and put the cards across the top of the board, in a horizontal row. The day I explain the new routine, Ariel is the line leader, and I tell her that her word can be something she loves or something she's afraid of or something she hates, but it should be something that's very important to her. She does not hesitate: "Mommy," she says. "I love my mommy." I write her word on a card and tape it under her name on the board. When it is Lily's turn, she chooses "fairy" and tells a story about a fairy with a hurt wing. We act the story out.

Children start to come to school on their day to be line leader with a word in mind, which they keep secret until our morning meeting when the word will be proclaimed.

Jasper is the exception to this general excitement. When it is his turn to be line leader, he has no words. Children suggest "marble roll" and "dog." He rejects their suggestions. The card under his name on the board is blank for several days while the spaces around it are filled by the important words of other children. Finally, I imagine to get me off his case, he chooses "cat." He can't explain why he wants that word or what is important to him about cats. Maybe he wants a word he knows he can spell correctly.

But one day, Jasper has a surprise for us: it is his turn to be line leader, and instead of murmuring "no" when I ask if he's ready to tell us an important word, he whispers, "Explode." He gives me his tiny smile, just the corners of his mouth turned up.

Later in the morning, I ask him if he wants to tell a story to act out about his word "explode." He says, "There's a man and a dog and a volcano. And the man takes care of the dog, and the volcano makes fire and explodes. A cover goes on top of the volcano. The end."

It is a very controlled explosion, but Jasper has found a word that has meaning to him.

A few days later, Jasper, Glen, and Keith are sitting around three sides of the table containing Lego cars, trucks, and workmen. Each boy has pieces of a construction vehicle in front of him.

"They're good guys," Jasper says. He picks up several little people. "Who wants guys?" he asks.

Keith takes one of the small construction workers, laying it flat on the table. "Look, he's dead," Keith says.

Jasper piles several people on top of one another. He works intently, trying to put a tiny gray backpack on one of the figures, and then he gives up. While Keith is working on his truck, Jasper takes back the figure he'd given Keith and puts it on top of his own pile. Keith, appearing not to notice, begins work on his second truck.

"Keith!" Glen says. "You better look out! Behind you! Lookat! Three makes six, so there's six on this!" He puts a small red piece next to Keith's first truck and touches it carefully with his forefinger. "Pshhhh! I blew it up!"

Keith ignores the destruction of his vehicle, continuing to work on attaching a front loader to the new truck he's building. Then he looks up, notices that the previously crowded block area is now empty, and says, "Hey! Let's go to blocks!"

Glen and Keith quickly leave their trucks and head to the block area, where they start building a puppy house.

"No one plays with me," Jasper whispers so quietly I would have missed it if I hadn't been standing behind him, eavesdropping.

"Do you want someone to play with you here?"

"Yes." Jasper emphasizes the ending; he never says "yeah," the way the other children do.

"Jasper would like someone to play with him at the Lego table," I announce, pleased that he wants to play rather than practice the alphabet and that he wants to be with another child, not alone.

Ben comes over, plays silently for a few minutes, and then leaves without a word, heading for the greater excitement of the puppy house.

Jasper collects all the trucks previously used by Keith and Glen, spreading them out in front of him. "Sh-sh-sh-sh!" He makes a softer version of Glen's sound as he gently breaks each one apart and puts the pieces in a pile.

"What happened?" I ask.

"They exploded," he says.

"Exploded!" I say. "That's your word, Jasper!"

He smiles, his dark eyes meeting mine for a moment before his gaze goes to the board, finding his word. Another smile, a little bigger this time.

I take a piece of paper off the shelf behind me. "EXPLODED!" I print in large letters. "That's an exclamation point," I explain, demonstrating the difference in the way I read "exploded" and "exploded!"

He takes the paper from me eagerly, holding it up so that all the children can see, first facing the block area, then the art table, and finally the drama area, like an actor accepting his applause. The children do not look up from their blocks, drawing, or pretend play, but Jasper carefully lays the sign on top of the pile of demolished trucks. Then, having anointed them with print, he picks up the paper, takes it to the story table, and trims off the white space around the word.

"Do you want to tape that on the wall next to the Lego table?" I ask when he returns.

"Yes," he whispers. He tears a ten-inch long piece of clear tape, carefully keeping his hands away from the teeth of the cutting edge of the dispenser, puts the strip vertically on his horizontal sign, and tapes it to the wall.

There's an important word.

∗ 17 ∗

No Animals in the Bank

"I want to be a deer!" Ariel's voice cuts through the block area play.

"Well, we're making a bank!" Glen answers.

"Yeah," Caleb agrees. "A bank can't have aminals in it. All it has is . . ." He pauses, trying to capture his next word.

Felipe, who can't stand to wait for anything, finishes Caleb's sentence: "Is a rhinoceros."

I look carefully at their structure: The base of their building is made of the largest size of hollow wooden blocks—each one is four feet long, six inches wide and deep. Next are the middle-sized ones, each a foot long by six inches, and on the very top are the smallest triangular blocks for decoration. The entire structure can easily enclose three or four small children. Inside one of the medium-sized blocks sits a small gray stuffed rhinoceros wearing glasses.

"Well," I say, "if there can be a rhinoceros, I think there can be a deer." I am quick to defend Ariel. She easily feels excluded, and when she does she tends to withdraw with an angry outburst, an extended pout, or both. Once that happens, it's hard to bring her back for a compromise.

"It can be a animal banker that works in the bank. He can get food by working there," Keith says. Keith is one of the youngest in this group. He is almost a head shorter and almost two years younger than Caleb, but Keith knows how to negotiate and keep a game running.

"What do you want?" Caleb says. "Let Felipe choose. Number two—you can choose. Number three—you can be a money banker."

Caleb may be starting his list with number two. His understanding of the constancy of numbers is shaky, and numerals are more like a memorized list than they are a way to understand the concept of number. But perhaps he meant that the first choice was to let Felipe choose. In either case, his suggestions seem to offer generous options for Ariel.

"I'll be a worker, then," Ariel says, surprising me with her agreeableness.

"My rhinoceros is going out to get rhinoceros food." Felipe apparently accepts her answer and moves on with his role in the game.

"I'm going to actually be an animal that works." Ariel makes it clear that she is compromising but is still a deer.

"Yeah," Caleb agrees, "but it has to stay in the building."

"Then I'm quitting," Ariel says, startling me with her unreasonableness just as she had surprised me one moment before with her flexibility. Perhaps she believes she is being slighted because Felipe can leave the bank to get food but she can't.

"OK," Caleb says, ignoring her. "Let's make a bank, guys! We're making a big bank."

Keith notices that I am watching Ariel, who has moved away from the block area, her head down and her shoulders slumped. We both know that loud wails are likely to follow soon.

"I said she could," Keith tells me, aware of my concern about her and defending his own behavior.

"Keith said Ariel can work inside," Caleb agrees.

"I agree with Keith!" Felipe says.

"Well, I don't!" Caleb suddenly changes his mind. "If it's only a human bean! Aminals stay out of the house. This is only for humans. When you go in banks—well, have you seen a bank with aminals in it?"

"Well," Keith says, "the rhinoceros is in the bank. He's even wearing glasses."

"Well, Ariel," Caleb says, "have you seen a aminal in a bank?"

Keith understands that if there is a rhinoceros with glasses in the bank, then we are not playing out a realistic scene, and therefore a deer might as well come in, too. But Caleb does not see this complexity. He knows he has a strong statement—"Have you ever seen an animal in a bank?"—and he uses it for each argument that comes against him.

"No," Ariel says quietly.

"But there was a rhinoceros in the bank," I insist.

"Yeah, I don't get it," says Felipe, the owner of the bespectacled rhino.

"It can only be a *stuffed* aminal," Caleb counters. It does sound like a logical argument, but it does not convince Felipe.

"I don't get your point," Felipe says. "Why could a rhinoceros be and nothing else?"

"It's just a difflience," Caleb says.

Keith stands up for Ariel again: "I've never seen a rhinoceros in a bank."

"Yeah," Caleb says. "Have you seen a rhinoceros in a bank? Have you? Well then. No such thing."

I believe that Caleb thinks Keith is supporting his statement "There's no animals in the bank." But Keith is actually supporting the opposite idea: since there's already a rhinoceros, we might as well allow a deer.

Felipe, at five, can keep the thread of his own argument clear throughout the discussion: if rhinos are allowed, deer should be, too. Keith, the youngest in this group of players, can take the argument one level deeper: if a rhino with glasses can work in the bank, then we are clearly in the realm of pretend, where you can be anything you want as long as it helps the play go smoothly.

Caleb quickly goes over to the supply shelf and takes a piece of paper and a yellow marker. Turning to the undisputed authority of the written word to add emphasis to his argument, he writes "NO" in large letters. He sits in front of Ariel's plastic tub that contains her crayons. "ARIEL," he prints, copying the letters from the front of her tub much more quickly than he writes in his handwriting book. I didn't know he could recognize her tub by seeing her name on the front. And I've never seen him write spontaneously before. He tears a long piece of masking tape off the dispenser and tapes the sign on the bank. "No aminals get in the bank," he announces. "Well, have you seen an aminal in a bank? I just don't get it." He echoes Felipe's words but with his own meaning.

The other children become very excited, seeing the new sign on the bank; even the children who thought Ariel should be allowed in begin to take paper, markers, tape, and copy his idea. Soon signs indicating "No Ariel" in bold Crayola colors are taped all over the structure as the excitement passes through the room like a bolt of lightning.

To be thrilled by the meaning of the written word—isn't that what I've been working on so hard this year: our growing list of important words, Jasper's sign "EXPLODED" that still hangs on the wall by the Lego table?

But now, with the word "NO" electrifying us with its power, I say, "Stop! Look at Ariel! You must take those signs down!" and begin the untaping.

Caleb looks at me angrily, then looks at Ariel, who is standing near the door, her hair almost covering her eyes, which, we all know, contain tears. He walks toward her. I edge closer. I never can predict what Caleb will say. He puts his arm around her. She lets him do it. He whispers in her ear, and I'm about to demand that he say it out loud.

But I don't because I see her body relax; she smiles and walks back with him to the block area.

* 18 *

Treasure Hunt

On most days, once the classroom is full of children, noise, and excitement, Jasper still retreats to the security of his lists. This week he's moved from his previous location, alone at a small table, to the busier life at the large round table where I sit and write the children's stories as they dictate them to me. This move provides him with easier access to the paper, markers, scissors, and tape that reside there, as well as to the conversation that takes place as children come and go, telling their stories.

"Does *eight* have a *g* in it?" he asks the first morning after his move. I lean over to look at his paper, where he is listing the hours of the day, beginning with "one o'clock" and "two o'clock." His new location facilitates these casual conversations.

A couple of weeks later, he is beginning a new list—the children's favorite words. I watch as he carefully copies the top row of words under the children's names, until he has written each child's first important word. He holds his pencil in the hammerlike grip of a very young child, but his printing is small, precise, and in lower case, just like mine: mommy, fairy, dog. He takes a pair of scissors and begins to cut around each word. Scraps of paper from outside of the words fall to the floor, and he does not stop to pick them up. A couple of cut-out words fall, too, upside down, and he does not look up from his work as I rescue them from the floor and put them carefully on the table beside him.

When he has written and cut out the first row of words, he begins to place them around the edge of the rug. "A treasure hunt," he announces softly. I am the only one who has heard.

Ten minutes later, we come to the rug to act out our stories. I'm not sure what Jasper expects will happen, but I am suddenly afraid that the children will not appreciate his plan and might even decide the scraps of paper belong in the recycle bin.

"Jasper invented a new game," I announce quickly. "Find the first important word from your own list and sit behind it for story acting." The children are delighted to see their own words in this new context.

"Let's do this again tomorrow!" Felipe says.

Jasper smiles at the floor as his new game makes connections between him and the excited children joining him at the rug.

* 19 *

Storms and Skunks

It is the day before winter vacation, and the first storm has just dumped eighteen inches of snow on the ground. At recess, children ages four through twelve build a fort that is big enough to hold dozens of them. All sizes of children roll huge snowballs, the biggest children put one on top of another, and the smallest children plug up the holes with handfuls of snow.

When we come back into our classroom, Caleb signs up to tell a story. "Once there was a big city and it had a lot of problems," he begins when it is his turn. "And the problems were, trucks and police cars couldn't get there, so the only thing was the tow trucks, because they helped the policeman get out."

Caleb still does not understand that he needs to describe the snow to enable his listeners to imagine the same picture that he has in his mind. Or does he have a picture in his mind? Sometimes I'm not sure his language process involves an image or event first and then words that describe it. It seems as though he starts talking without a clear idea of where he's headed.

"What was the problem with the city?" I ask.

"Because there's a big storm and everything got on the city."

While I write, I am already imagining how we will act out this story, one of the most logical he's told. I picture Caleb as the tow truck and all the other children as cars stuck in the snow, waiting for a turn to be rescued.

"Everything got on the city?" I write his words, but my inflection contains a question. I assume I know what he means by "everything," but I want him to explain it more clearly.

"Nobody can get past," he says, "'cause there's too many skunks—

they're spraying around their tails. The firemen put water on the skunks," he continues, happily. "He goes near the skunks and tears them off."

I don't ask him to explain about tearing them off. If I hadn't asked what got on the city, maybe he wouldn't have gone off on the skunk tangent.

Caleb has just turned seven. I have an important question to present at the first staff meeting after vacation: Can our small school, with its community that accepts differences, continue to meet his needs? Or should we recommend that he go to a school for children with learning disabilities? I am hoping that we can keep him, but I believe that he needs to learn to speak coherently before he can learn to read. Can we give him that time?

I plan my presentation. Caleb has made major strides in several areas. He now plays well with other children—when he first arrived in my class he had ordered others around, oblivious of their need to have a part in planning the script. He put children in imaginary jails, handcuffed them, and allowed them out only at his own whim, often without checking first to see if they wanted to be the bad guy in his story. Now he can incorporate their ideas into his plot, using his knowledge of each child's favorite characters to entice them to join his game. He has begun to listen to books I read to the class, joining discussions about what has happened and what might happen next. He is starting to understand that each letter has a corresponding sound, and to remember some of them. When the line leader chooses an important word, Caleb can sometimes think of another word that begins with the same sound.

But unlike most of the children, he does not recognize his own list of important words. Copying letters is extremely difficult for him. And what concerns me the most is his confused stories—a snowstorm that turns into skunks and requires firemen to save the day. How will he be ready for first grade, which includes a writing curriculum in which children are expected to write both fiction and nonfiction? If I can convince the rest of the faculty, my main goal for him this year will be to tell coherent stories, both real and pretend.

I know the first-grade teachers feel pressure to have all their children reading quickly, and I know that Caleb cannot accomplish this complex task if he does not arrive at their door with a list of common words he can recognize and the letter-sound relationships firmly established. I am afraid that the first-grade teachers will disagree with my recommendation that Caleb should learn to speak coherently before we worry about letters and beginning sounds.

The week after vacation, I come to staff meeting armed with Caleb's stories, pictures, and writing. I describe his strengths and his difficulties. I read his story about storms and skunks to the group, emphasizing his progress in language and social skills but also the areas where he's far behind—his stories that change direction midstream, his inability to recognize his own list of words, and his difficulty completing a math project.

"What he really needs," a first-grade teacher says, "is a tutor who will teach him language the way you do a toddler—finger plays, rhyming, repetitive stories, nursery rhymes."

"Counting the steps to the school!" another suggests enthusiastically. "All the simple activities he didn't get as a toddler, when he should have been learning language."

We have just such a tutor on our staff, an aide at the school who is finishing his training as an Orton-Gillingham tutor, taking a multisensory approach to teaching reading to learning-disabled children. We agree that he will give Caleb intensive language tutoring throughout the school year and then start to work on reading during the summer. In September Caleb will begin first grade, and a year from now we will reevaluate his progress to decide if we can keep him.

I'm thrilled with the unanimous support of the teachers for this plan. His mother, who believes that our language-rich school is the best place for her son, is also willing to support our plan. I feel like I've been rescued by a friendly tow truck.

∗ 20 ∗

Drumming

Hushed, excited talk fills the air as we file into the gym and see the four drummers, dressed in African tunics and headgear, with their large West African dundun drums. As one of the youngest classes, we get front-row seats on the floor.

Our school's location, far from a city, makes it hard for us to attract as diverse a population as we would like, so in our annual Martin Luther King assembly we try to celebrate other cultures by bringing in storytellers, musicians, or artists from around the world.

As the drummers begin to play, they choose one child at a time to come up to the front of the gym and join them at the drums. I always dread this choosing of a child—I may end up with one delighted one, but the other fourteen are resentful and disappointed that they did not have a turn. At last, though, the leader looks at our space on the floor—and chooses Caleb, whose head has been bobbing to the music since the opening beats.

I worry if he's up to the job. During group discussions he still tends to be a bit off the subject. He cannot follow multistep directions. Up in front of the whole school, how will he know what to do?

But he shines his joyful smile and stands behind the drum, confident, as though he's been doing it all his life. The lead drummer shows Caleb the hand signs for starting and stopping. Caleb, who never pays attention when I give directions for a math lesson, starts exactly on cue, and his hands move to the beat throughout the song, his whole body joining the rhythm. When the leader makes the hand signal to stop, Caleb, amazingly, is watching and his hands become immediately still. The drummers keep him with them for the rest of the program, and he takes a bow with them at the end.

I am delighted at his success but embarrassed for my own secret worry. Why should I assume that he would not be able to watch for the signal to stop drumming, just because he doesn't hear my directions for finding the numbers that add up to 10? What does staying on the subject of a group discussion have to do with staying on the beat of an African drum? If he had been raised by his Roma family, would he have become a musician, with no need to read or write? Schools demand certain skills—sitting in chairs for long stretches, paying attention to subjects that are often of no interest to the listener—skills that are often not required in other areas of life. I don't want to get caught in focusing on disabilities only to forget strengths.

After we return to class, I wait to see whether the unchosen ones are resentful. Whether it's because Caleb was so good that they feel he deserves the honor or whether it's because of his frequent generosity and kindness to others, no one complains.

21

Caleb's Rules

1. You Can't Say

I decide that at snack time I will bring up an issue that has been troubling me for a while. "I noticed in the block area today that Ben was told he had to stand guard outside the puppy house while everyone else was inside," I say as we sit around the rug eating and talking about the morning playtime. I want to tell the children to be kind, to ask how they would feel if they were told to be the only outside guard, to remind them of the Golden Rule. But I remind myself that the children almost always figure out rules that are fair and more meaningful to them that any rules I impose, so I restrain myself.

"Yeah. They wouldn't let me come in." Ben agrees with my assessment, his head low. Our rule "You can't say 'You can't play'" protects a child like Ben, on the low rung of the social order, from being kept out of the game, but I have noticed that when the roles are given out, he is given the least desirable.

"Not everybody." Caleb quickly defends himself in case I was accusing him of being unfair.

"It's always Ben who's supposed to stay out," Shawn says, agreeing with my assessment. "And all the other people get to go in."

"Yeah, you're right." When Caleb hears Shawn's honest description, he stops being defensive and takes responsibility. "'Cause we shouldn't have done that."

"What do you think Ben should do if that happens again?" I ask. In the past, I might have demanded that the other children change their behavior toward him. Although this seemed to work for a little while, they reverted to their old behavior when I was out of earshot.

So I began instead to encourage the group to help and support the underdog.

Ariel answers tentatively. "Maybe I can say, 'You can't say you can't go out'?" She knows what it's like to be told to do something she doesn't want to do in a game.

"Ariel!" Caleb says enthusiastically. "That's a new rule! You can't say you can't get out!"

"Do you mean that you don't have to do something in a game that you don't want to do?" I ask. "That would be a good rule to practice when we go out to recess after we're done with snack."

Caleb loves rules. Although he may forget to follow one, especially when he is involved in pretend play, he likes to remind others to follow them, and he would like to invent new ones. He recognizes "You can't say" as the beginning of a rule, one that will help a child who feels left out. But like Ariel, he does not understand that a rule is a larger idea that contains many smaller examples. "No touching when you pretend to fight" is a useful rule because it includes no hitting, no biting, and no pushing. It encompasses both intentional and accidental aggression.

"And my rule!" Jasper says excitedly. "You can't go out without a teacher!"

"Well," Katya says, "that's not the kind of rule." She understands that the main idea of this discussion is exclusion, not rules for safety.

She may be right, but I want to support Jasper's first venture into the realm of group discussions. "Jasper's is a different kind of rule," I say. "It's an important safety rule."

"Oh, yeah," Caleb says. "Because if you got lost in a fire. That's the kind of rule." His example may not be quite logical, but it is about safety.

"You can't go outside because you might get hurt or stealed by bad guys," Katya says, giving a clearer example.

"If you get hurt," Shawn agrees, "there would be no one to help you."

"If there's a bad guy broke in this school," Caleb says, "it's easy—call 911."

2. No Breaking Bones

My heart sinks when the teacher who has been on recess duty walks toward me as my children line up at the door to come in. She's not likely to be bringing good news. Sure enough, Caleb, Katya, Jasper, and Glen are in trouble.

"We pushed Katya down," Caleb confesses as soon as I ask what happened. "We were Power Rangers."

I appreciate his honesty, but briefly I wonder if I should keep this group in from the next recess, imposing consequences that will ensure that next time they remember the rules. But will that help Caleb learn to express himself clearly? Will it help him learn to play safely when a teacher or parent is not supervising him so closely?

Caleb continues: "You know what? A new school rule! If someone's on the back and they try to get him down, and they throw him down on the back, that would really break his bones!"

"You're right, Caleb," I say, noticing his attempt to make a rule that would prevent this from happening again. "You can't throw people down because that could really break a bone. We have a rule that says 'No touching when you pretend to fight.' So that includes not throwing people down. Remember the rule that says you have to be two arms' lengths apart?" I hold my arm out in front of me. "You hold your arm up, too." Our fingers almost touch as I demonstrate the distance required for shadow boxing. "That way you can't accidentally hurt each other. If you forget that rule, the teachers at recess will probably tell you that you can't play the Power Ranger game," I warn.

"But you have to remember, you two," Caleb tells Glen and Katya. "And me. And Jasper."

"They didn't push me all the way down," Katya says. "They just pushed me half down."

I realize from her tone that she does not feel she has been hurt or mistreated. If I had not listened to the details of the interaction, I would not have gained this important information.

"So nobody was angry?" I ask. "You just forgot the rule?"

"Yeah, yeah," Glen says. "We forgot the rule."

"Next time, could you remind each other," I say, "so no one gets hurt and your game doesn't get stopped?"

"OK," Glen says. "We will."

3. Snake Rules

Jasper, Felipe, and Ben are building in the block area in the morning when Caleb walks in carrying a five-foot-long red-and-black plush snake with a tongue that goes in and out when you squeeze its head. They come over to admire it.

"Don't even go like this," Caleb warns, wrapping the stuffed animal around his neck like a scarf. "He'll squeeze you right in the neck. You suffocate, that's the worst part."

"That means you can't breathe," Felipe says. "It's really dangerous."

"Who wants to help me build the cage?" Caleb asks.

"Me! Me! Me!"

"I want to, too," Ben says. "Don't forget about me!"

"How about you, you, and you, Ben," Caleb says, including all the boys who volunteered but making it especially clear he is including Ben. "All we have to do is start using drills."

"Drills! Yeah!" They each go to the block shelf and come back with a block that is six inches long and an inch in diameter. Loud drilling begins as they hold these small blocks perpendicularly against the big blocks.

"OK, Shawn," Felipe says, "do you mind being alone guarding the cage?"

"No," Shawn says.

"Hey, Jasper," Caleb says, looking at the blocks Jasper had been using earlier, "can we take this down?" When Jasper doesn't answer, Caleb kneels down next to him. "Guys! Be quiet!" he says to the drillers. "I have to hear! Can we take down this whole building?" he asks gently.

"Yeah," Jasper says. "I'm not using it."

"Guys!" Caleb says. "We're taking down this building! Be careful! OK, guys. Now the rules are, don't put your hand in like this because he'll bite you." He puts his finger in the snake's open mouth to demonstrate the danger. "Number two: He'll suffocate you. Number three: This kind of drill is powerful."

Don't put your finger in the snake's mouth, don't put it around your neck, and be careful with the drills: three safety rules, in numerical order, all understood by his friends. Caleb's wish to communicate in play is making his language more logical and clear, reassuring me about my decision to help the children figure out their own rules for safe and fair play.

4. You Can't Play

I am on recess duty when I see a big group of boys starting to get into a physical tussle at the other end of the playground. I round them up and bring them over to the picnic table to talk. "I wasn't really fighting," an older boy from another class begins. I go over the details of what happened, remind them of the rules, and give them my usual warning: if they can't follow the rules, they will not be allowed to play their superhero game.

"You can't say 'You can't play,'" Caleb tells me.

"You're right, Caleb, that's another important rule," I say.

"No," he says. "*You* can't say 'You can't play.'"

Now I see what he means. "I think I was saying 'You can't fight,' not 'You can't play,'" I tell him.

"Oh," he says, thinking that one over. "Right."

* 22 *

The Secret Key

"Caleb was fighting with two other children," the recess teacher tells me, bringing him into my classroom, her hands on her hips, her voice full of exasperation. Caleb is by her side with his shoulders tensed and his chin up defiantly. "They were starting to punch each other," she adds.

When jackets come off in the spring, there is always a burst of new energy; the children seem taller and more exuberant, and we have to reinforce the rules for safe outdoor play. But punching, even then, is unusual.

"I called them over to talk with me," she continues, "and I reminded them of the rule—you can't touch each other when you pretend to fight. Then Caleb started to argue with me."

"Well, that's what the school is!" Caleb interrupts. I look at him, puzzled. "Touchstone!" he says angrily. "That's the school's name. Ya know—touch! The school should change its name 'cause it says 'touch stone' and that means touch, and why does it have that name if we can't touch each other? It's a stupid name and I'm not coming to this school anymore!"

On one hand, Caleb is being a boy in the spring, looking for any excuse to justify his burst of energy and impulsiveness. On the other hand, it is typical of his use of language to focus on a literal interpretation of a specific word or to use a word in his own way. I remember my daughter, at a much younger age, worrying that when I said I would "drop her off" at a friend's house, she might literally be dropped.

Is Caleb's idiosyncratic use of words a result of a lack of spoken language in his Romanian orphanage? Might he have had untreated ear infections that affected his ability to hear and understand language, just as he had an untreated cold or respiratory infection when Golda picked him up from the orphanage? Even so, most children from international adoptions acquire functional, age-appropriate language skills within six or eight months after they are adopted into a language-rich environment.[1] It is still difficult for Caleb to explain himself clearly to others even though he has continued to receive speech therapy and is in a classroom full of language. My challenge is to try to help him use his increasing language skills to explain to his friends how he wants to play a game or to tell a teacher what happened when something has gone wrong.

"I'll take care of this," I tell the recess teacher, knowing Caleb will never back down while she is in the room. Her expectations for his behavior are reasonable: he needs to know that he must not fight in the playground. I wish that he could talk with her about what happened. At this point, though, without a relationship with her he will only feel criticized and defensive.

I am concerned about Caleb's increasing aggression. Until this spring he's behaved well, which makes his learning difficulties manageable in our school. But recently he's been joining in the most aggressive games on the playground. When the play becomes too rough, a teacher intervenes. Then Caleb starts to argue, insisting that the teacher is wrong. If only he would be contrite, say "I'm sorry; I forgot," and "I'll try not to do it next time," he would quickly be set free, let out of the verbal net in which the teacher constrains him, and could return to fantasy, where he controls the prisoners and holds the key to the handcuffs.

This year I can protect Caleb by intervening quickly when he has a conflict. I have learned, by trial and error, that if I remind him that I like him and I'm here to help him, he can let down his defenses, look at his mistakes, and learn from them.

But it is April, and in June he will enter a remedial summer program where he can begin intensive reading tutoring. I don't want him to be seen as the "bad boy," or worse, kicked out for his aggres-

1. Miller, *Handbook of International Adoption Medicine*, 389.

sion. I have two more months to help him learn to talk coherently when he's made a mistake, even with a teacher he doesn't know well, instead of trying to fight back in a battle he can never win. Although he needs clear limits, I believe that punishing him for his mistakes at this point would only drive him into withdrawal, making it less likely that he would learn the skills that will help him.

I suspect that today he already feels attacked twice—first by whoever threatened him in the game and then by my colleague's understandable irritation with his attitude. I will have to help him back down before we can talk about the problem.

After the recess teacher has gone, we sit down at the art table. "Caleb," I say quietly, "do you remember the stories I told about Abe Lincoln—how he told the truth even when he made a mistake?" I pause, giving him time to absorb Lincoln's strength. "Tell me what really happened outside."

Caleb's shoulders relax. "We decided to play a game of robber— Jasper and me and Ben." He pauses. "That's all."

This is clear, as far as it goes, but it does not include the conflict. "When did the fight start?" I ask. "The one that upset the teacher."

The defiant edge returns to his voice. "I don't have to really, really, really listen to . . ." There is a long pause. I could tell him that he really does have to listen to the teachers, but this would stop the conversation. Caleb knows he's in the wrong.

"When did the fight start?" I ask again.

"Because we just got mad at each other," he says.

"Why were you mad?" He looks down at the table, silent. I remind myself that Caleb doesn't answer "why" questions. The concept may be too abstract for him: most likely he does not know why he behaves the way he does. I try again. "Who were you mad at?"

"No," he says, thoughtfully now. "We weren't mad. We were just pretending mad."

"So did you forget the rule that says 'No touching when you pretend to fight?'" I wonder whether another boy's pretend punch came too close and threatened him.

"Yeah," he says. "Guess what. Well, guess what?" Caleb starts talking quickly now, without his previous hesitations. "That teacher made Jasper feel sad when she yelled at us. So that's why I got into that argument with her."

Was Caleb trying to protect Jasper from the teacher's anger? My image of the altercation changes as I am reminded of the many times I have seen Caleb protecting and helping Jasper: I picture Jasper on the day he was inconsolable when he didn't get a turn to play with his favorite tub of Legos at quiet time, and I remember Caleb bending over him saying gently, "Jasper, Jasper, it's OK, 'cause when I see them and I pick 'em out, I'll give 'em to you, OK?"

Caleb is the oldest in the class, while Jasper is the youngest. Regardless of Jasper's superior skills in reading and writing, Caleb looks out for Jasper and comforts him when he's upset, like a protective older brother. I remember that Caleb's mother told me that in his orphanage, at age two and a half, he helped take care of the babies.

"Caleb," I tell him now, "it's so important that you tell teachers what happened when they want to talk with you about a problem at recess. You know why?"

"Why?"

"Because then the teachers will know how kind you are. If you don't tell them, they won't know that you wanted to help Jasper when he was sad. The teacher might even get the wrong idea and think that you're rude."

"I get mad, you know," he says quietly, "when I have to get in trouble."

"I know that," I say, making my voice as gentle as I can to offset my stern message. "But everyone else in your game is still outside playing, because when the teacher talked to them, they told the teacher they'd stop fighting. You're in here because you acted like, 'No, you can't tell me that.'"

"But that 'No' sentence," he says, "I was just trickin' about that from her . . . Hey! I have to ask you a question: Can you trick teachers? Can you?"

I think he means, "Do you teachers know how I really feel, underneath the bravado?" It's an interesting question, but I'm starting to formulate a plan, and I think we'd better stay on the subject.

"Here's what I want to do," I tell him. "When a teacher says, 'What's the problem here?' or 'What are you doing?' I want you to try to tell her exactly what happened, just like you told me today. Then I'll send a note home to Mom, so you can practice explaining it to her." I see his frown reappear. "I'll tell Mom not to be mad at you," I say. "This is for practice, to help you stay out of trouble so you won't get mad. She can help you make a plan for what to do if the problem comes up again."

It's a good thing there is no "zero tolerance policy" at our school. I think it may be a long time before Caleb can totally curb his impulse to defend himself when he feels threatened. But if he can explain himself to his friends and to the teachers, he can learn to talk about conflicts when they come up and avoid some of the more serious consequences of his impulsive behavior.

The next morning, an opportunity to try out my new plan appears. Katya comes running up to me at recess. "Caleb kicked me," she complains. It is a big step for Katya to come for help instead of fighting back, and I know she needs me to take Caleb's aggression seriously. At the same time, Caleb needs me to be supportive. A couple of months ago I might have been annoyed at Caleb's behavior, feeling frustrated that he was not making progress more quickly. But now I remind myself that it will take a long time to undo the damage caused by his early experiences. And if there is damage that cannot be undone, I must be patient, teaching him to deal with his limitations.

Caleb has his back to me, perhaps hoping trouble will go away if he doesn't see it coming, perhaps steeling himself against my expected assault. I walk toward him slowly, trying not to look threatening, taking Katya with me. "Caleb," I say, "remember how you're going to practice telling the teachers what really happened? I need your help so I can understand this problem."

Caleb loves to help. I hope he'll accept this idea.

He turns toward us and looks at Katya. "Well, I didn't want to be tagged, so I kicked her by accident. But I really didn't mean to kick her."

"What were you playing?" I ask.

"Katya was a horsie," he says.

"I held his hands behind his back to handcuff him," she explains. "He was a bad guy."

Katya, almost two years younger than Caleb and with a traumatic history of her own, knows intuitively which information I need most in order to understand the important aspects of the conflict. It's easy to take this ability to see a situation from another person's point of view for granted, until you see the struggles of a child who is unable to do it.

"We were trying to steal," Caleb adds. "Well, not *really* trying to steal."

"You were pretending to be a robber and Katya was the policeman and she was putting your hands behind your back to put handcuffs on you and put you in jail?" I say, trying to explain how this all fits together.

"Then I fell," Caleb says.

There's the attack. "Is that when you kicked her?" I guess, imagining he felt attacked by this unplanned accident.

"Uh-huh, because I wanted to get out of jail."

Now it's easy to picture how Caleb felt trapped, even assaulted, by her action. Perhaps if I can get the whole story after each incident on the playground, I'll find that Caleb's aggression is always such a clear reaction to a perceived physical threat. If so, maybe I can help him to understand this and eventually to use his verbal skills to respond constructively to the situation.

"Now we need to make a plan," I say. "How can you play this game without anyone getting angry or hurt?"

"I know!" Katya says. "I'll pretend there's a secret key and Caleb sneaks up and gets it." She begins to whisper as she shows how Caleb could tiptoe up, take the key, and unlock his own handcuffs, escaping from the imaginary jail. "And he opens the door and then he puts it back in my pocket." She replaces the invisible key in her own pocket, as she plays both characters in the scene.

"That's a great plan," I say. "Let me see you both try it." They act out the scene together.

"Now you know, Caleb, that if it ever happens again that someone pretends to put you in jail and you want to get out, don't kick. Just pretend there's a secret key and let yourself out." I don't know if he can use this idea of a fantasy solution in another conflict, but it's worth a try.

"Use your words," Caleb agrees. "Don't kick. That's much better."

* 23 *

A Little Bit Scary

"Once a baby kitty climbed up the lamp and she hurt her paw and it got broke," Katya tells me. "And then she had to get an x-ray. There's a mom who takes care of the baby, and the baby has to get a cast because she had to have a lot of food to make her feel better." As I write Katya's story in her notebook to act out later in the morning, I realize that she is eating better at school these days and her lunchtime upsets are less frequent. I wonder if having two lunchboxes has helped her feel more in control around eating.

"*No. This is *my* game." I am interrupted. Puzzled by the sound of an unfamiliar, gravelly voice, I look up quickly toward the block area, where I see Caleb, Ariel, and Felipe facing Jasper, all of them standing outside a house of large blocks that encloses most of the rug. I know the voice does not belong to Caleb, Ariel, or Felipe. Looking at Jasper, I realize I have never heard his voice at loud volume before. He is asserting ownership of the game, and no one is disputing his claim.

A child is the "boss" and can say "It's my game" when he or she came up with the idea, suggesting, "Let's pretend . . ." If others are convinced to join, they implicitly agree to his leadership and will usually go along with his plans. The punishment for any unfair decisions is that the other players quit, leaving the game's owner with no one to boss around. In the future, that child will have to come up with a new and exciting idea to entice others to try again. It's an effective leadership training system, rewarding both fair play and inventiveness.

I finish writing Katya's story and walk over to the game. "Well,

Jasper said we were going to Haunted Island," Ariel says. She speaks fast and paces nervously around the rug.

"Who are you pretending to be?" I ask the group. I tend to jump in quickly when either Ariel or Jasper is involved.

They tell me that Caleb is the owner of a motley array of pets: Felipe is a bull, Jasper is Robot Dog, and Ariel is a puppy. "I'm afraid," Ariel explains. "The owner's gonna take us to a haunted island and I don't want to go."

"You don't want to go for real?" I ask.

"It's not for real."

"I know." I try again. "But you really don't want to pretend to go to Haunted Island?"

"I really don't want to!"

"Caleb," I say. "You're her owner and she really doesn't want to go. What can she do?"

"Maybe she could go in the house and be safely in there and the others could go to the haunted island," Caleb suggests.

"Yes!" Ariel agrees.

"We can go to Puzzle Island," Jasper says. "It won't be scary. Just a little bit scary . . . I can block things that are scary!" he adds.

Not only can Jasper can block scary things: he can also be a boss who listens to others and suggests a compromise.

"I'll stay home," Ariel decides, going back inside the safety of the block house while Robot Dog and his crew head off for new adventures.

* 24 *

Little Peep

In my school mailbox, between a catalog for science equipment and the agenda for Wednesday's staff meeting, I find a book: two white pages folded and stapled in the middle, making eight sides. The cover proclaims the title:

LITT

EL

PEEP

The letters fill the page, with the middle E backwards. Caleb's printing is improving, but lines are written over several times, and where the vertical and horizontal segments should touch, they often overlap or miss the connection.

Caleb's new tutor, Phil, has begun to work with him each day for a half-hour. We have two main goals for Caleb: we want him to be able to tell a fictional story with a beginning, middle, and end, with consistent characters and a plot, and to be able to tell a personal narrative, a true story about something that happened to him, that is coherent and logical. Caleb's personal narratives tend to be disjointed, and his stories wander from one set of characters and one plot to another. Before he can learn to read, his spoken language skills must be developed enough so that he can understand the meaning in the story he is reading, and before he learns to write he needs to know what information the reader needs in order to understand his communication.

Each day, Caleb tells a story, Phil writes it down in a small, stapled book, Caleb illustrates it, and then they act it out together. This process is cementing their relationship, a necessary precursor to working with Caleb: he is so afraid he is stupid that he must trust his teacher will not be critical when he makes a mistake. When they act the story out, Caleb gets immediate feedback on what information he needs to add in order to allow Phil to understand and dramatize the images in Caleb's mind. He gets this feedback without criticism, without being told his story is not good enough.

I open the book to the first page:

"Little Peep was in the forest."

Phil has written the words along the bottom, and Caleb has drawn Little Peep in pencil on the top half of the first page. Peep has an oval face, two eyes, a mouth with jagged lines for teeth, a square body with legs, and a long tail. There is a row of arrowlike trees diagonally across the page. This picture shows tremendous progress in Caleb's ability to draw a representational and recognizable figure—until recently his drawings were scribbles just beginning to turn into simple forms. Although I cannot tell what kind of animal Little Peep is, this picture has details that fill out my understanding of him and his environment.

"Some people got him for keeping."

The person next to Little Peep is huge, with an open mouth larger than Peep's whole head. Peep is smaller than on the first page, looking scared and powerless. Coming from his head are the letters N-O. The N is to the left of his head and the O is to the left of the N, making it look like "ON," but I am sure that Caleb wrote the N first and then the O next to it. Peep is screaming out, resisting capture.

"And then they put him in a cage. He was scared. He said, 'hoo.'"

Peep's eyes are now slits; one is partly open and the other is closed. His mouth is a zigzag of fear. A rectangular box with a lock encloses him.

"Then he was shaking from fear."

Peep is small, walking sideways, with a jagged line behind him showing his fright. Caleb, who rarely expresses emotion directly, has drawn a nightmare of terror.

"Then he knew they weren't going to hurt him. They just wanted to keep him."

Peep is smiling, his eyes open now. He is still enclosed in the rectangle, but now small lines cross-hatch his cage, like rays from the sun or the bars of the cage opening.

"Then he wanted to stay here for the whole time because he liked the place."

Still enclosed, Peep is larger now, with a smile that covers half his face.

I wonder if Caleb could have told this story, ending it so clearly, without help. Later in the day Phil comes into my class while the children are at gym. "Tell me about the story of Little Peep," I say, wanting to know what role he played in the dictation. "It's so much more expressive and more coherent than most of his stories. Did you help him with it?"

"All I did was listen to his words and write them down," Phil says, "one sentence on each page." He puts his big notebook on the little round story table and sits down, looking like a large but gentle bear on our small chair. He opens the notebook to a page full of small, tidy writing and rereads his meticulous notes. "Then he went back and drew the pictures, asking me, 'What does this say?' on each page. When I started working with him, his pictures didn't always correspond to the words, but now they do. He understands we need to read the words on each page in order to know what picture belongs there.

"And another thing that's important," he continues, "is that this story doesn't change direction at the end."

"Did you stop him there?" I ask. "Or did he know it was the end himself?"

"He just stopped," Phil says.

"It's a wonderful story," I say. "I think it's the first time I've heard him tell a narrative that has a beginning, a conflict, and a resolution. And it's also the first time he didn't go off on a tangent—either with new characters or a new plot—somewhere during the sequence." I'm thrilled that he's so quickly meeting one of our goals, and I wonder whether the one-on-one experience with his tutor will carry over to the classroom.

"This idea of being scared and being safe comes up over and over again," Phil says. "Somehow it connects with his adoption story."

I read the story again.

Little Peep was in the forest.
Some people got him for keeping.
And then they put him in a cage. He was scared. He said, "hoo."
Then he was shaking from fear.
Then he knew they weren't going to hurt him. They just wanted to keep him.
Then he wanted to stay here for the whole time because he liked the place.

"Caleb was taken away twice," I say. "First he was taken from his birth family to go to the orphanage, and then he was taken from the orphanage to be adopted. That feeling of being taken, being afraid, and then being cared for is so beautifully expressed here, through Little Peep.

"Did you act the story out?" I ask. Dramatizing his stories, with Caleb taking his favorite roles, is the part of the process that helps him to see what the listener needs to know in order to make the written description match the scene in Caleb's imagination.

"We did," Phil says, checking his notes. "He chose to be Little Peep, and I was the one who caught him and put him in the cage. Then, after I read the line 'He wanted to stay here,' Caleb changed the story. He said, 'Then I ran out.'"

"Oh," I say. "So he didn't stop at the end after all?" The story was so complete the way it was, and now Caleb seems once again to have been off on a tangent.

"I wonder why he did that," Phil says.

In my disappointment that he may not have met my goal, I forgot

to wonder about the meaning of his words. Now I imagine Caleb
acting out the part of Little Peep, experiencing the capture, realizing
that even though his captors aren't going to hurt him, he's still not
free. "When he acted the story out as Little Peep," I say, "he could
feel that being caged is not as good as being free, no matter how
kind his protectors are." Maybe Caleb, as Little Peep, wants to grow
up and be independent.

25

Fire!

"We gotta build the whole thing back together!" I hear Jasper tell
Glen early one morning.

"You get out first, then I'll get out, then you'll get back in, OK,
Baby Eeyore?" Glen answers.

I wonder whether Glen's question implies a change in the balance of power between them: he seems to be listening to Jasper's
opinion, and he is asking, not ordering.

"Pretend there was a hot room and we're coming through it!"
Glen continues.

"I have to go there quick!" Jasper agrees. "Oh."

There is a crash of falling blocks, and I look up from the art table,
where I am pouring finger paints into small jars. "Is everybody all
right?"

"Yeah," Glen says.

"Easy," Jasper adds.

"This is gonna be easy to build up," Glen says, clarifying Jasper's
answer.

"We can fix this."

"That's simple!"

The children do not share my concern about bumped heads; they
only want to be sure the hot building can be properly reconstructed.

"Ah! Baby Eeyore! Ah! Go for cover! Quick! We're mountain lions!" Glen says, roaring.

"We are melting lions!" Jasper says, perhaps thinking of heat intense enough to melt him. Changing from Baby Eeyore to any kind
of lion poses no problem for players who are experienced in pre-

tend, where motorcycles are transformed into chairs for the band at a moment's notice.

"Me and Jasper are the two mountain lion chiefs," Glen says. Again I note a more equal balance of power and wonder which of the boys is learning more from this early morning arrangement. Has Glen missed Jasper's verbal error, or did he choose to repeat the correct word rather than to laugh at Jasper's mistake?

"The innovator! The innovator! The innovator!" Jasper calls out. I do not ask him what he means. I am learning, too.

"No, no, no!" Glen responds negatively to Jasper's idea, although it seems unlikely that he understands it.

But now Jasper insists. "We need to put this here!" he says, holding a long block.

"Well. Jasper," Glen says, preparing to dismiss his idea.

"This is a elevator," Jasper explains, correcting his word substitution and adding the block to the building.

"You're a mountain lion!" Glen gives a reason for his rejection of the elevator.

"Yes." But Jasper does not back down or move the block.

"Can I play?" It is time for school to begin, and Caleb and several other children have come into the room. Most mornings, this is the point when Jasper quits the game.

"Yes," Glen says. "We are being mountain lions. We're a rare kind."

"Why are so many people playing?" Jasper asks.

Glen ignores the question. He likes the block area when it's full of his friends. "This is a really hot room!"

"It's burning, Caleb!" Jasper suddenly turns up the level of excitement in the game while he accepts Caleb's entrance into it. "It's gonna fall!"

"It's about one hundred in here!" Glen elaborates on Jasper's statement. "It gets hotter by the second!"

"We have to do something!" Jasper agrees. He goes to the nearby story table, where I have already put out paper, tape, scissors, and markers. He takes a piece of paper and writes something. I walk by trying to look casual. This is the first time I have seen Jasper combine his love of writing with his new skill at pretend play. I read:

Cant Go in tihs Room

it fier

I notice he is taking risks with his writing, even putting down words he has not practiced. He picks up a pair of scissors and holds them upside down, with his thumb in the large hole and fingers squished in the small hole. He cuts around the words carefully, tears a piece of tape, and puts his sign on a block at the top of the burning building. "There's fire inside this room," he announces.

"I can swim in water." Glen, not yet a reader, ignores the sign. "It's really hot because only the water team can go in here. Know why? 'Cause they can turn into ice or water!"

But one of the children, transforming into water or ice, bumps the blocks and they come down with a crash.

Jasper finds his sign in the rubble. It has been torn almost in half. "Oh, no! It's ruined!" he says.

"We can fix it," I tell him.

"Now, look!" Jasper says, holding up the torn sign. "I'm gonna do something else." He walks away from the game and sits down at the story table, taking a piece of blank paper from the tray.

In the two months they have been playing together in the mornings, Glen has begun to listen to Jasper's ideas without dismissing him, letting Jasper influence the direction of the game. Jasper has become more confident in his ideas and begun to cope with the noise and commotion as children negotiate constantly changing characters and plot.

Today Jasper stayed in the game while children joined, the plot changed, and blocks fell down. Only the disappointment with his torn sign convinced him it was time to leave.

I know he'll be back. The lure of mountain lions and burning buildings has become too powerful for him to resist.

* 26 *

Uncle Caleb's Time Out

"Music is stupid," Caleb announces loudly as we line up, ready to go.

Caleb usually enjoys our weekly music class. Last week, I peeked in the door to see him marching proudly as the hunter in *Peter and the Wolf*, stepping crisply to the beat, imaginary rifle over his shoulder. I am pretty sure that music is not the issue.

As the children head into the music room, I whisk Caleb aside, before he has a chance to get defensive. "I don't want you to get in trouble in music class," I tell him, putting my arm around his shoulder. "So let's talk about this first." I pause, but he stares silently at his gym shoe, the laces dragging on the floor. I want to fix it for him, but since he thinks he should know how to tie, he prefers to pretend to do it himself, making a stack of half-hitches into an impossible knot.

"Mom told me you said good-bye to your Uncle Caleb this morning," I tell him when it is clear he is not going to continue the conversation.

He looks up, startled. "How do you know that?" he asks.

"Your mom sent me an e-mail."

"You know the sign that comes up at the beginning of a video?" he says. "The FBI warning? It tells you not to make copies. He made copies of movies. He was like a pirate on the computer. My mom says he went to time-out." Caleb pauses. "I'm seven. I know that really means he went to jail."

Although Caleb's language can still be confusing, I understand the idea. But without his mother's description of the Internet piracy and one-year prison sentence, I might have wondered if it was one of Caleb's fantasies.

How can Caleb understand that the man who went with his

mother to Romania when she adopted him is a bad guy who needs to go to jail? Young children see issues of right and wrong in simplified terms: people are either good or bad, the police and robbers of Caleb's fantasy play. In a few years, once the basic rules of behavior and morality are mastered, they can begin to understand that all of us contain mixtures of impulses and actions. Caleb, with his restricted ability for abstract reasoning, is getting a crash course in these subtleties.

"I feel sad," he adds.

This is the first time I can remember hearing Caleb describe himself as having a strong emotion.

A few days later, Caleb's mother sends me a story he dictated to her. It's called "Uncle Caleb's Time Out."

> Everyone in my family was angry and upset. At first I thought I had done something wrong. I felt really bad. Then my mom told me today was a sad day for our family. My Uncle Caleb was going away. My Mom said it was like a time out for adults. A judge sent him to time out, to think about what he did, I suppose.
>
> The day Uncle Caleb was leaving, I tried real hard not to cry. When Uncle Caleb hugged me and said goodbye, he was crying. This made me scared. I was afraid I would never see him again. Or maybe someone would take me away. I lie in bed at night and get sad thinking about Uncle Caleb. Where did he go? Was he missing me? Was he still crying? Was someone hurting him?
>
> I miss him a lot. I think about him during the day when I'm at school. Sometimes I start thinking about Uncle Caleb and I feel sad. This makes me angry with other people.
>
> My mom told me when I start to feel this way I should talk to my teacher. She understands kids' problems.

I assume that in writing this down, Caleb's mother edited and organized his words. But the thoughts and most of the language are clearly his own.

The following Monday, he comes to school a half-hour late, finds it hard to sit still during our meeting, and barely eats at snack time.

At the end of recess, as the children line up to come inside, Caleb's friends report to me that he has yelled at and insulted them and would not stop when they asked. He refuses to come in, and I get an aide to read a book to the other children for a few minutes so I can talk with him.

"I saw Uncle Caleb in jail," he says, beginning without his usual pause, as though he had been waiting to tell me. "There's no bars on the windows because he didn't do something dangerous."

I wait to see if there is more. "It was good to see him; I was scared," he adds quietly.

"We have to go back to the classroom," I say, "but I want to help you so you don't make your friends mad at you. Do you want to take some time alone? You could draw in the cubby room until you feel more settled, and I'll tell your friends you want to be alone for a while."

"Yeah," he agrees.

A few days later, Caleb's mother sends the next section of "Uncle Caleb's Time Out."

On Saturday, we visited Uncle Caleb. He is thirty-one hundred hours away in a state called Pennsylvania. I was really scared. The person at the desk told me to quiet down. I couldn't help it; it was hard. I was scared and excited about seeing Uncle Caleb.

On Sunday we visited him again. I tried my best to act appropriately and I did.

I wonder briefly whether Caleb actually used the word *appropriately*, and I decide he probably did—he loves big words and now more often uses them correctly.

It felt really good to see Uncle Caleb. He couldn't come to the car with us.

On Monday, I told my teacher I saw Uncle Caleb. I still felt sad and kinda yelled at some kids in the playground. That made me feel worse. Then my teacher talked to me and I felt safe.

Uncle Caleb will be away for a long time. Mom says it is a year. Mom *tells me it will be over before you can blink your eyes. All I know is this is a hard time for my family and we feel sad a lot. Mom says the good part is we can all feel sad together as a family. Some people don't even have that.*

I hope when I open my eyes from batting them, Uncle Caleb will be home. We can go fishing. Maybe skateboarding!

As I read his story I begin to see that Caleb is engineering a three-way conversation—telling his mother what happened in school, listening to her, and using her suggestion that he talk about his feelings with me.

Using language to communicate important information, understanding what another person needs to know in order to comprehend his story, knowing that communication can help him plan and make hard times better—that's what I wanted for him this year.

Maybe now he is ready to begin to learn to read.

* 27 *

They Played

"There was a dog," Jasper says, sitting at the story table. "Put number 1 right here." He points to the first line of the page, and I write as he directs:

1. *There was a dog*
2. *and another dog*
3. *and another dog*
4. *and another dog*
5. *and another dog*
6. *and another dog*
7. *and another dog*
8. *and another dog.*
   And they played.

* 28 *

A New School Year

Jasper, who has not yet had his sixth birthday, is in my class for a second year, while Katya and Caleb are both older and have moved on. Our school has several multiage classrooms, so staying with a teacher for a second year is not considered unusual.

Jasper likes to arrive early each morning so he can start building before the louder, more dominant boys arrive. This morning, before school, Katya has also come to visit me, and when she sees that Jasper has built a three-sided block structure with a large piece of cardboard for the roof, she decides to join in.

"It's a doghouse!" Jasper tells her. "We can both fit in it! Make it even longer!"

"I will," she tells him, handing him a long board that is three feet long and six inches wide. He sets it down as the fourth side, leaving space for a door.

He looks at it. "Only one person can go in it," he decides.

"Well, we need more blocks then," she says. "Look, I'm making it extra good." She enlarges the enclosed space by adding two more blocks to the length on each side.

"The roof's not high, now," Jasper tells her. "If it's not high, we'll make it a little more upper."

"Now that <u>would</u> be good," she agrees. "Watch what I'm gonna do." She removes the cardboard roof and adds blocks to each side. "Then the roof can go higher," she says, replacing the cardboard on top.

"You couldn't have done that," he objects. "They'll all fall down. It's *my* thing. *I* made it."

How I love the sound of those proud, demanding *I*'s. "That's pretty good," Katya says, admiring her own work.

"You don't do it like this—it has to be *very* high. Take the roof off," he orders. "It won't be high enough."

They remove the roof again and build the sides still higher.

"I think we're gonna do it," Jasper tells her.

I think so, too—and Jasper is going to join the boys who rule the block area, taking control of his own buildings, while Katya will accommodate when she needs to, taking orders as well as giving them.

* * *

Caleb's first-grade teacher comes to me eagerly at recess, holding a ragged paper. The top half of the page is unlined, with space for a drawing, while the bottom half is ruled for big printing. The drawing shows two large heads on stick bodies, tears pouring from their eyes in straight dotted lines. Two straight-line arms stick up from one of the bodies, and at the ends of the arms are circles. A larger circle goes around the two smaller circles, Caleb's depiction of handcuffs. His printing on the bottom half of the page has a great variety of letters all strung together with no spaces, and under it his teacher has written a translation:

"My uncle got put in handcuffs. When he got to jail, then he got put behind bars. Then he thought about the things he did. He thought about if the police would take him away. They took him to the higher jail."

I had heard that Caleb's uncle might be taken to a new prison, farther from his home and more difficult for Caleb and his mother to visit.

Looking more closely at Caleb's printing, I see that his letters correspond to the beginning or emphasized sounds of most of the words. Not only does he know the letters and their sounds, but he is also able to listen to the words as he says them, putting down the letters that seem to fit most closely to what he hears.

"The best thing," his teacher tells me, "is how excited Caleb is about this. Yesterday, first thing in the morning, he asked me,

'When's that writing time?' And when I went over to see what he was doing during writing workshop, he was stretching out the words, listening to the sounds, and writing down the letters he could recognize. He sees himself as a writer now!

"I know he has a long, hard road ahead," she continues more slowly, "but he's so motivated!"

And so is she.

Caleb has consistently been able to reach out to those who care for him, beginning at the orphanage, where instead of being rejected as a low-caste Roma, he was chosen, at age two, to help care for the babies, and where his caregiver was so sad he was leaving that she couldn't come to say good-by.

A few days later, I see Caleb in the hall, coming from the bathroom. "Hi," he says shyly, glancing into my eyes for just a moment.

"How's your new class?" I ask him.

"Great!" he says.

"What do you especially like?" I ask.

"Everything!"

One quick intake of my breath contains a wisp of sadness that I'm not a part of his new success, or maybe it's a touch of envy of the teacher who will be with him for these new steps.

"I'm so glad," I tell him. I give him a hug, and he softens into it for a moment.

"But I liked your class, too," he adds. He gives me a quick smile and heads into his classroom, a little skip in his walk.

Epilogue

1. Caleb

The secretary apologizes: she's sorry but Golda's on the phone. Would I like water or coffee? It's two years later, and Golda is squeezing in my interview before leaving for her annual trip to the Vineyard. As I finger the furniture fabric samples in a box on the chair next to me, I remember how Golda chose her child from the video and imagine Caleb enjoying the adventure of leaving at three in the morning to be on the ferry by dawn.

Once Golda greets me and we head into her office, she gives me her full attention. For the past year, Caleb has been attending a school for children with language difficulties. I ask Golda how she made her decision to send him to a school for learning-disabled children rather than keep him at our school and have him tutored.

"It was in January, the year after he left your class," she tells me, "and I had been thinking about whether to keep him at the school. He told me that he couldn't do the math and he was stealing Glen's papers and he was copying them. He was crying, and I said, 'Why do you do it?'

"'He said, 'He's a smart guy!' So I went to the teacher, and she said Caleb couldn't do the math without help.

"I was so upset—it's like you thought school was going OK and now again the problem is rearing its head. You want it to go away!

"I said to Caleb, 'Look at me! I dropped out of high school because I had so many learning disabilities. You've just got to pick yourself up and do it. That doesn't mean you're gonna be a rocket scientist! But who cares! Most of those people can't tie their shoes!'

So you know, you do what you have to do. It's so important to focus them while they're young."

I ask her about his new school, and she shows me a brochure:

All (our) students have language challenges as their primary disability. Their language deficits have limited their ability to learn, and as a result, many have previous histories of school failure. Students arrive at [the school] working at least two grade levels below what their age would dictate. For the most part, these students are dependent learners, i.e., they do not learn from their environment or pick up skills from watching others. When they enter [the school], students cannot use reading as a functional tool to learn. In addition to their language problems students often have visual, perceptual or motor deficits, significant social and self-esteem issues, and often have attention deficit disorder, or other secondary disabilities which interfere with their ability to learn.

I picture Caleb at a school where all the children have difficulties reading and writing, so he does not stand out as different, and I like that image.

"I went to see this school he's at now, and I said, 'My god, this is so different! This is so rigid!' And it's an inconvenience—it's not easy to get there. You know, learning disabilities are not like physical disabilities or autism. You can pooh-pooh learning disabilities. But I knew I couldn't just continue with what I was doing. 'Cause I was paying for school, I was paying for tutoring, I was paying for speech therapy. I was paying twenty-seven thousand dollars a year. And he was failing!"

First, Golda had found an advocate to try to get the public school system to pay for his school. The advocate said the public schools would never pay for it; she should pay for it from her own pocket.

"I got a new advocate. We met with the person who was going to run the program in the public schools. They were telling us what they would do for him in their school, and they were trying to tell us it would work for him to go there instead. And I said, 'Where's the program?'

"'We don't have it.'

"'Where is it?'

"'We're going to make it up.'

"I said I want to see the program, and they said the program was in their heads and that they had no funds but they would make it work.

"I was like, 'I don't think so.'

"The advocate did her thing and she said, 'OK, it's time for a lawyer.' Now we have a court case coming up to make the public school pay for the school he's going to because he needs to be there. I think they will pay for it eventually."

Golda believes that the new school is a good choice for him because he is so learning disabled. He has been diagnosed with auditory processing disorder, dyslexia, and attention deficit disorder. Golda tells me she has heard about studies linking ADD to early malnutrition.

"So now we know—he just can't control himself. He was on 30 milligrams of Ritalin, and he was having some side effects. We tried him on a new medication and we literally had a monster on our hands. We took him off medication for a week—he was on nothing—and the school called me and said if he wasn't on medication he wouldn't be allowed to attend the school. He can't sit still. Now he's on a small dose of Ritalin—20 milligrams. We lowered the dose and it was much better. Maybe next year he should be on 25 because he's growing. At the end of the year he was having some focus issues. Each day he gets a report on how he did in each class that day. They give you blue sheets for anything they do extraordinary and incident reports if there's a problem. Caleb got one incident report because he wanted to know what it felt like to get one. He was talking in class—talked back to the teacher. The incident report means you don't have recess and you have lunch with all the other kids that had incident reports.

"He hates it. He wants to go back to Touchstone. He's a whiner! He's just a whiner! 'I miss my recess—the recess is too short!'

"I said, 'Well, get on the student council and complain about it then. I don't have any power. I'm not going to call them up and complain—that's your job!'"

"How's his schoolwork?" I ask.

"He's doing good. He struggles; he works hard. He complains all the time. But it was a good decision; it was a good decision. We read together a lot. He just struggles. And he tries so hard. And he does the math. And it's hard for him. It's just hard. Even talking—he wants to get something out, but it's so hard for him. So even though I wish he didn't have to be there—I wish I could drive to the best public school in the city and pick my son up at the end of the day—but it ain't gonna happen. It ain't gonna happen."

Caleb is now reading at the first- or second-grade level. He uses a word processor instead of handwriting. He feels good about science and social studies—he seems to be at a higher cognitive level, Golda tells me, where he is able to understand more complex ideas.

"You know, he's getting older. I see him with his friends, and they're doing multiplication and stuff, but he's doing probably second-grade work. He's nine and a half. He's doing addition, subtraction. He feels good about what he's doing. His handwriting is a mess a lot. But I am adamant—he hates doing homework with me because I make him do it over: 'Do it over; that's the end of it, and you know it's for the best for you.' He says, 'I know.' When I see employees that do a job that's not complete, it's because nobody pushed them. And he needs to learn it now because he has learning disabilities. So he needs to be better than the guy who has the 150 IQ. Because he's not going to get anywhere on his cognitive abilities. He's going to get it on his tenacity, on his persistence, on his personality and work ethic. So it is the right decision, but it's still hard to accept. You just want the best for your kid."

Golda shows me the letter she sent to his camp counselors this summer:

This is an introduction to my son Caleb, who will be attending your camp this summer. I thought it would be helpful for your staff to understand Caleb's learning difference. My goal is to make Caleb's camp experience a positive one and educate your staff to the situation. Please keep in mind that learning differences are not a mental illness, mental retardation or autism. Many successful and famous individuals have struggled with ADD and dyslexia—Winston Churchill, Albert Einstein,

John Chambers, Henry Winkler, Thomas Edison and General Patton to name a few. I have enclosed an interesting article on the subject.

Her letter goes on to describe Caleb's learning difficulties, giving specific examples of how they might show up and how the camp staff could handle them appropriately. At the camp, Caleb had spent a week on a schooner sailing around Cape Cod and had a wonderful experience.

Golda takes out a photo album. Her search for Caleb's Romanian family had finally succeeded, and she shows me photos of his uncles and cousins; one cousin looks so much like Caleb that I have to remind myself that it couldn't be him—he was not in Romania when the photo was taken last summer. I see their bleak yellow house behind a broken fence, surrounded by large puddles of deep mud and water.

"I put together a book of photographs for his birth mother. The person who located her took a picture of her looking at it." Golda shows me the letter and then the photo of a woman with Caleb's dark hair and prominent nose, tears in her eyes, looking at the photos. Before seeing these pictures, I had wondered how Golda would know whether the woman was really Caleb's birth mother. Seeing the photograph, I am convinced.

I remember Golda's long search for his birth mother and ask why she felt it was so important to find her.

"Well, I didn't do it for me—I did it for him. I just felt strongly because I've read that adoptees that weren't given that opportunity—every single one of them said there was something missing. And I felt strongly about it. Number one, the woman who gave him up—it can't be easy to give up a child—I don't care who you are. Number two, this is not about me—it's about Caleb feeling a connection somewhere. Because when you sit at our table at Thanksgiving, nobody looks like him! I saw an article in the paper recently about a man who was seventy and his mother was almost one hundred, and she just told him he was adopted! He felt cheated. He felt like it was a lie. And I don't want my son to feel like there's something that's a secret. When there's a secret or something that you don't address, it's something bad; it's something negative. Put that together with learning disabilities—I mean, I'm headed for problems!

"And maybe I'm sensitive to it because I, as a kid, was in so much trouble. I felt so strongly that this was his right to know. I think he needs to know his roots. I heard there's more teen pregnancy among adopted kids, because if you can't see your roots you create them."

Golda plans to take him back to see his birth family someday, when he shows an interest in them. For now, he is sad that they're so poor and sad that he was taken away from them, but he does not want to go back.

"I feel it's something that if you can, you owe it to your child," she explains, "just like an education. A lot of parents put their head in the sand and don't do what they should do, whether it's getting services, looking for birth families. I just think it's that old adage of wait and see—it's ridiculous. I was in the same boat when I first adopted him. I didn't realize—these kids are different."

"Did you want to hide your head in the sand?" I ask.

"No! As soon as the doctor said that to me, I was all over it. Of course you want to! Nobody wants to have a child that's different—you just worry about them. But that's not life. That's not the right way to do it. Because I know what happened to me when I had a disability. I dropped out of high school because I had so many learning disabilities.

"Caleb's are severe. They will interrupt him having a good quality of life. If I hadn't gone to that doctor, I probably wouldn't have known for a couple of years. You know, he's going to be something! I don't know what! But oh, man, I hope he's not a police officer—I'll shoot myself!"

I wonder about the intensity of that exclamation and decide that her own past as a school dropout and a teen in trouble probably left her suspicious of law enforcement.

"People say, 'Would you do it again?' Probably not. I told them at the adoption agency point blank I don't want a child with learning disabilities. I'm not capable of handling it. Somebody thought I wanted it, I guess! I was thinking of a second child, but I chose not to. What if I had a second child with learning disabilities? I'd shoot myself; give me a break! I've had enough kids.

"But I can't think of a time without him—he was my kid from the time I saw the video."

2. Katya

Halfway down the long driveway through the woods to Robert and Lynn's house, I am welcomed by Jake, a large mixed-breed dog with the brown, white, and black face and the floppy ears of a Burmese mountain dog. As I open the car door, he asks to be petted and is commended for not jumping on me. "Good dog," Robert says as he comes out of the house to greet me.

Lynn's e-mails all end with her signature quote, "May I be the person my dog thinks I am." I see her point: Jake assumes I will be as happy to see him as he is to welcome me. Lynn, I suspect, may prefer dogs to people, just as I generally choose to spend my time with children rather than with adults. Robert, on the other hand, is as welcoming to visitors as Jake is. Would I like coffee, fruit, anything else in the house? We sit down to wait for Lynn, who comes in shortly.

"I went for a walk," she explains. "When I came home from dropping Katya off at camp I needed to cool down. I'm not going to go to the liquor store and grab a six-pack, so I'm going to take myself for a walk. She's driving me nuts, and it's happening all the time."

This is not what I expected to hear: when I see Katya chatting happily with friends in the hall on the way to gym or running with a crowd outdoors at recess, she seems increasingly settled. She is now eight years old, and it's been a long time since I've heard the old accusations that she's making a friend feel left out or being too bossy in a game. I had expected to hear that things at home were going well.

"What was it like this morning?" I ask.

"In the morning she's digging her heels in from the minute she wakes up. She wants to go to camp, but everything's an obstacle. This morning the sneakers weren't right. One lace was broken. Very simple: take the laces out of her other shoes. No, she didn't want to hear about it. 'Then we'll be late for camp and everybody will know I'm late,' she says.

"I'm like, 'Katya, we're already an hour ahead of schedule. I'm never late with you.' I prepare for an hour of this. And eventually she decides to do exactly what I said a half-hour before, and I look at her and I say, 'Gee, that was a really good idea you had, Katya.' But it's like everything was wrong this morning. The toast was wrong. The butter was wrong. The bacon was wrong."

"Is there a problem with camp?" I ask.

"I think a lot of this right now is connected to eating," Robert says. "At summer camp no one keeps on top of her to get her to eat and drink. So at the end of the day, she's a bit dehydrated, and she generally had nothing to eat except for some junk food that she got at the camp store. And when she's completely exhausted at the end of the day and hasn't had anything to eat and can't even handle herself, she doesn't want to do anything, she doesn't even want to leave; she says, 'You don't have a play date for me after camp!'

"Yesterday I picked her up in the afternoon, and she's been having trouble afternoons after camp, so I wanted to do something that she'd love. So I said, 'Let's go get Chinese food together,' and I was expecting 'Oh, great, Dad!' But what I got was 'I'm not going anywhere. You never let me bring a friend along!'"

I'm reminded of naptime at her day care center: if she had a playmate nearby, she would wake up without screaming. I wonder if she still feels safest with her peers and most threatened by the love of adults.

"I have to say," Robert continues, "that food has been a constant theme with Katya from the day we first saw her at the orphanage when they were force-feeding her gruel. And then we got her home and she was underweight and under height."

"She couldn't stop eating," Lynn adds. "Then she leveled out, like all other picky kids."

"I remember how hard it was for her when she first came into my class." I say.

"It was hard for her to settle down to eat because she was too busy," Lynn tells me.

"She would open her lunchbox," I say, "and be mad at whatever was in there."

"We take her to the grocery store," Lynn says, "and she picks stuff out and then she doesn't eat it. Now last night, she chowed down her Chinese food."

"But it was unbelievable getting her to the point where she would take the first forkful," Robert says.

Like any two parents, Lynn and Robert may have slightly different views of Katya's development. Robert tends to connect her challenging behavior to her early deprivation and trauma, while Lynn more often sees it as a difficult but normal part of her development. Is it important to decide which view is more accurate?

Perhaps what matters with a challenging child like Katya is finding some way to step back from the conflicts she brings up and regain the empathy for her that allows the adult to find more patience. Robert tries to understand her behavior in relation to her past experiences. Lynn goes for a walk to regain her own equilibrium. For me, imagining what it would be like to be a toddler in that orphanage and feeling how that experience might affect a five-year-old helps me put Katya's behavior in perspective and imagine a solution for her lunch problem. In whatever way we do this, increasing empathy allows us to take a longer view of Katya's development—to be more patient, less quick to feel frustrated by her, and more tolerant of our own inevitably imperfect skills as parents and teachers.

My thoughts return to Katya's present-day social adjustment. "How are things going with her friends?" I ask.

"Getting play dates has been problematic," Robert says.

"People have kind of paired off into little groups where they have their own kind of constant play dates," Lynn agrees.

"But we're suspicious that there's a carryover with the parents from the time when Katya was quite a bit more rambunctious," Robert says. "That reputation has stuck. So she conducts herself well now—when she's at other people's houses she's polite and helpful. I think the kids want to play with her outside of school or camp, and these kids ask their parents and the parents refuse to call back or constantly have one reason after another why it's 'no.'"

"Is there anything you think Katya might be doing to make it more difficult, or is it all left over from old times with the parents?" I ask.

"Well," Lynn says, "there's two friends, one boy and one girl. She wants to play with them, and they were friends before Katya knew them. And Katya comes in to rock the boat, and she happens to be an in-your-face kind of kid and the girl is shy. She just wants the security of that old friend. So the parents have said, 'We were doing fine without Katya. Let's get her out of the picture.'"

"Are there other friends where this isn't a problem?"

"Yes, yes. There are other kids. But she really wants to be with those two. She's had a lot of pain with it this year," Lynn says.

"Are there areas where you've seen change?" I ask.

"When she was in your class, we started the behavior management plan that our therapist recommended," Robert says. "We counted to three, and if she didn't behave she got a five-minute time-out. We got some level of success with it. There was a while when she actually started timing herself out before we gave her a time-out, and she'd come back OK."

"I did it this morning," Lynn says. "Now she'll yell and scream at us throughout the whole time-out or cry through it and fall asleep. But these episodes today are infrequent. What's around more is her just digging her heels in. She has made progress at realizing she self-sabotages sometimes. She can now reflect back on a situation and say, 'I should have had something to eat' or 'I should have had some quiet time.'"

"She's better at calming herself down when she's excited," Robert says. "She said, 'Dad, you can say to me "Calm, calm," and that would work.'"

"Does it?"

"It does, sometimes. Then when it doesn't work, she says, 'You always say that to me!' But I think my attitude is changing. When she was in your room, it was like there was this thing to be fixed.

Now I'm starting to think of it more as this is Katya and this may be something that defines her whole life. Perhaps, hopefully, her natural self-control will improve over time. Or her skills for recognizing what she's doing will improve. I'm starting to think about what the whole impulse control and excitability thing might mean for her in the future. I mean for her, the slightest touch could send her into laughing hysterics that take a long time to calm down. I'm starting to accept that a lot of this is her, and some of it will improve, but there will always be an element of it here."

I'm reminded of my feeling that I had to be more patient in my work with Katya, that I was going to have to come to terms with my own wish to "fix" things for her.

"She didn't have the process of being stimulated and being soothed and being stimulated and being soothed," I say. "And being stimulated and discovering that she could soothe herself by sucking her thumb or her toe or moving around—to wait a few minutes until somebody came to take care of her. She missed that in her first years."

"I remember when we first saw her in the orphanage," Robert says, "the slightest little upset would produce a tantrum where she was on the floor, flailing around, punching the floor. It never occurred to me until you just said that, that she didn't have the opportunity to feel what the in-betweens are like, the result of gradually feeling soothed."

"Maybe her best chance of getting fed, if she was really left on the street, was to scream," I say, "not to be patient and suck her thumb. Maybe that's why she's alive today." I stop here and remind myself that although this kind of speculation can help us to be empathic and to come up with ideas for how to help Katya, there's also a danger in making these assumptions. I remember Gwen's anger at me for jumping to conclusions about Jasper and remind myself that there are many possible explanations for any behavior we see in Katya now. Challenges like hers are not found only in adopted children.

"Here's something wonderful about Katya," Robert says after a pause. "When new kids or visitors come, she's welcoming; she's helpful. She befriended a new boy who came into her class in the middle of the year, and they both have a real love for their guinea pigs, so they get together and have guinea pig play dates and make movies and stories about the guinea pigs."

Academically, Katya is making good progress in reading and is self-motivated. "She just went through a phase where she tore through a series of phonics workbooks by herself. She didn't want anybody to help her. Now she reads for her own pleasure—not to impress anyone or get anything. And she picks stories that make her happy: she started on chapter books recently—she reads the American Girl series. She likes being tutored, also."

"Why is she being tutored?" I ask, surprised, since she's enjoying reading a series that is appropriate for her age level.

"She was having trouble engaging when a new activity started," Robert says. "Let's say it was listening to a story or it was listening for the directions when she's getting ready for a new project. There was always this delay, and then she looked around to mimic what other people were doing."

I remember how she used to focus on her relationships with her friends, rather than on my agenda, and wonder if this was an attention issue.

"The educational psychologist who evaluated her thought it relates to temporal and sequential issues—things that have to do with time, sequence, and order."

"Which makes sense," Lynn adds, "because we were noticing that when she tries to describe or explain things, she leaves out the little words that connect the story logically together. She'll confuse before and after, she'll get them backwards or she'll leave them out altogether. And past tense was very late in coming—it's getting a little better."

The educational psychologist suggested that since Katya is so strong visually, the teacher supply visual cues to help her make connections. Her tutor felt that she may have auditory processing issues. Robert, who teaches dyslexic children, was considering taking her to an audiologist trained to look for those issues.

"But then I thought about what they do for these kids, and there's really nothing that makes that much of a difference. It's an issue of giving her the time to soak something in. So maybe after she hears the directions, she needs a little extra time to think about it or to write down what she heard or to watch a demonstration."

We are finishing up our conversation; Lynn gets up to walk Jake, and I am gathering my papers, thinking about the ups and downs of being Katya's parents, starting with that long trip bringing her home.

"While I was driving here today," I say to Robert, "I was remembering that plane trip with her from Russia. I was wondering what was it like for you. Was it just 'How am I going to survive?' or 'Oh, my god, did I get the wrong kid?' or was there no question—you had made this commitment and already she was yours?"

"There was this moment where I had gone into the galley in the back of the plane with Katya," Robert says, "and the flight attendant was trying to help me find a place on the floor that was secure for her where she wouldn't hurt herself. And Lynn was in her seat up front, and after I'd been gone for quite a while she had come back to see what was going on and she saw how scratched up and bit up I was, saw how distressed Katya was, and Lynn started to turn gray and green and she sort of semi-fainted or passed out, and I sat there and I remember tears came to my eyes and I went, 'Oh, my god. How am I going to handle this? I've got a kid and a wife who are both really, really distressed.' I remember this total exhaustion at that moment and crying a little bit, and that was a big emotional release. But I never for a second regretted picking Katya up and bringing her home.

"Was she already ours? No question."

3. Jasper

On the hottest day of summer, I walk up the steps into the cool and soothing climate of Gwen and David's house in a subdivision near our school. Both Jasper and his younger sister, Kalli, are at camp, and I am eager to hear how Gwen and David feel things are going for Jasper, who is now seven years old. At school, he does not run up to me with a hug or with news of his family and friends. When I greet him, he manages an uncomfortable hi and sometimes a fleeting glance. But I've heard from his teacher that he is doing well; he's an outstanding math student, he has made good progress in reading comprehension, and his ability to write a coherent story has expanded. I look forward to hearing more details.

As David, Gwen, and I settle on comfortable couches with mugs of coffee, Robert, Katya's father, enters without the formality of knocking on the door. He gives everyone a hug and sits down to join us. Knowing that all three sets of parents are friends, I have left it to them to decide whether to talk to me together or separately, and as Gwen and David welcome Robert into their living room, their ease together is evident.

"We had Jasper assessed in the spring," David begins. "He scores very high in pattern recognition, mathematics, and concrete reasoning skills, but he has almost no emotional vocabulary. On the TAT test, where they show a picture of a boy with a violin and you have to come up with a story about what the boy is thinking and what is happening, he would come up with some random story about dogs and cats playing. It had absolutely nothing to do with the picture. His ability to empathize is basically nonexistent. The closest comparison would be to somebody with Asperger's disorder. But it's not Asperger's, and it's not auditory processing disorder. If you give him facts, he processes at the same rate as anybody else. His ability to recognize word lists and make associations is fine; he's able to do that."

"It's when there's an emotional context or a story context and you've got to put it together into some sort of beginning, middle, and end and provide an emotional plot to it, that he seems to have trouble putting it all together," Gwen adds. "And he learns his social skills by rote, and we still have difficulty with that. If his friend Glen comes over, I'd say, 'Jasper, Glen is here.' Glen would be at the front door and Jasper would say, 'OK,' and he'd be just as likely to then go outside and play on the jungle gym by himself as he would to come over to Glen and say hi. So we had to go through the process step by step: when your friend arrives, you come to the door and you say hello, and you wait for him to come in, and you go somewhere with him. Well, now it's very rote, and so when a friend arrives, Jasper comes to the door and says the same script. He brings them inside and he waits. And you see him processing, 'Did I get to the end of the routine?' And once he has, he can ad-lib a little bit. But everything has to be taught to him. At camp, he does not know how to join a group at all. He loves to play foursquare, but he'll walk around and wait for one of the counselors to come and help him join. If his best friend were there, he would just go right up to him as if no one else was there and say, 'What are you playing?' and kind of blend in as if he were an extension of his friend; that works fine.

"The person who tested him says he's really PDDNOS, 'pervasive developmental disorder not otherwise specified.' It's kind of like saying we don't know.

"She also said he has an ADD look to him. When he went for testing he was picking up pencils, spilling them on the floor, couldn't focus for anything. She would test him for fifteen minutes and he would get restless. So I would take him down to the lobby and make him run up and down the steps and do jumping jacks, and then I'd take him back in. Then he could focus again. He can focus better than anybody I know, but he looked classic ADD on the day he was tested."

"But his teacher thinks things are going well?" I ask.

"Yes, he's doing well in school. His reading comprehension is much better."

"Sometimes after I read him a bedtime story," David says, "he'll say, 'Let's do comments and questions,' just like his teacher does in school after someone reads a story."

"When he reads by himself, though," Gwen says, "he'll open a book and read words. He doesn't read pages, and he doesn't read them in order. And he doesn't read sentences. He'll flip around pages and find words he likes. Today he was reading a Bunnicula book, and I said, 'Oh, what's that about, Jasper?' and he said, 'Isn't this a cool word?'

"But now he's been picked at his karate school for the leadership training program. He goes in twice a week, and he works with the younger kids—like three years old—and for a while all he would do was kind of mill around the outside and pass out lollipops at the end. Now his instructor has started having him be the chaser in the tag games. Yesterday he paired Jasper up with a little boy to show him how to do blocking. Jasper said, 'Go like this' and the little boy just looked at him, and Jasper got a panicked look, like 'Now what?' and the teacher came over and said, 'Now you take his hands and you put them up,' and he showed him how to do it. I can't think of anything better for Jasper."

"Is he pleased about it?" I ask.

"Oh, beyond pleased. This is the ultimate. And he'll get a special uniform that says 'Leadership Training' on the back."

"These karate teachers know how to do it," I say. "Maybe I should just run my kindergarten like a karate class." We laugh, imagining the principal's surprise at my announcement.

"The karate teacher knows that he has to say, 'Jasper, pay attention,' when he wants him to listen to something. If there's too much talking, Jasper's OK for the first sentence, but by the second sentence he's behind. So he checks out and he says, 'OK, I'm not part of this.' When his karate instructor talks to Jasper, he always sits down on one knee, right in front of him, but if he's across the room he always says his name. Jasper will rivet to his name and then pay attention.

"If we go to a birthday party, say at a gymnastics studio, and they say 'Everybody do this thing,' I can tell when it's too much for him; it's coming too fast, there's too much going on, he can't hear it. So I will always go up to the instructor and I'll say, 'That's my son; he can't hear well. So if you're going to give him instructions, you need to look at him so he can see your face, and please don't make him go first because once he watches the other kids, then he gets it.' And as soon as I say that, people go 'Oh, OK.' And I think, 'What kind of mother am I, telling people my kid's deaf and he's not?' But if I tell them he has a hearing problem they understand and they know what to do."

"In my conversations with parents of internationally adopted children," I say, "language processing keeps coming up as an issue. I've read that malnutrition and the lack of verbal stimulation might be causes of language processing problems. But Jasper was not underweight and under height the way Caleb and Katya were, and he had a caregiver who talked with him, didn't he?"

"Learning difficulties are more frequent in internationally adopted kids—there's plenty of evidence to support that," Gwen says. "And all three kids—Jasper, Katya, and Caleb—didn't have good prenatal nutrition. In fact, all three see a pediatric dentist, and the first thing he comments on is that the enamel on their teeth is not growing properly because their prenatal nutrition was poor."

"Katya has a hole in her molar now that you can literally look through; her enamel is soft," Robert says.

"You have had both an international adoption and a domestic adoption," I say to Gwen and David. Jasper's younger sister, Kalli, often comes into the classroom for a few minutes in the morning when Gwen drops Jasper off at school. Kalli seems unlike her brother in many ways—she's fair-skinned and strong-willed and loves to chat with adults. "Obviously, Jasper looks different from you while Kalli could be your biological child. Does that affect the adoption process?"

"I think there is a difference," Gwen says, "but I don't think it has to do with their physical appearance, because there are so many mixed families now. I think the difference is that a lot of domestically adopted kids are now the product of open adoption, and that's a huge difference. Kalli, at four, knows her birth mother; she talks to her on the phone about once every couple of months. She'll tell you the whole story—she knows her birth mother couldn't take care of a baby, but Kalli has very positive thoughts about her. It just occurred to her this year that there's something called a birth father, too, and she finds that bizarre: she says, 'I have two mothers and two fathers.' And she just found out that her gym teacher is pregnant. She came home and she said, 'Mom! Guess what! My teacher's having a baby—and she's keeping it!'

"Jasper has no clue whatsoever where he came from. And to the best of our knowledge, everything we were told is a big lie anyway. You need to understand that internationally adopted children come with varying degrees of connection to their homeland. Lots of times 'adopted kids' are viewed as one group. People will say, 'My cousin is adopted, so I get it.' But a child who is adopted domestically and openly deals with a whole different set of issues than the internationally adopted child, like Jasper, who has no information at all. This is a difference that will impact the child's willingness to address adoption, and perhaps it will impact the parents' willingness to disclose adoption-related issues openly."

"Are there any other things you've learned that might be helpful to parents and teachers?" I ask.

"One thing," David says, "is that adoptive parents are probably more sensitive, nervous, and protective of their kids than I think biological parents are. And as a result you've got to have that filter, with an adoptive family, that these parents have worked unbelievably hard to bring these children into their lives and they are very much invested in making sure that their kids are being treated correctly; maybe they're hypersensitive sometimes. I might not want to make a generalization, but adoptive parents could easily get labeled as problem parents because they're very demanding of their kids, very demanding of the teachers—very, very demanding parents because they are scared a lot of times. And it's not that they are afraid you're going to do a bad job; they're just really protective of their kids."

"What are they scared of?" I ask.

"They're scared that their kids are going to rebel against them; they're not going to love them because they're adopted. They're scared that they're going to be viewed as less competent parents because they're not biologically related. There's all kinds of issues that adoptive parents face, maybe not consciously but maybe subconsciously, that make them a little bit more protective and a little bit more sensitive as parents."

Robert joins in for the first time. "I think we're scared that we're going to miss something in our child's development that a biological parent wouldn't even have to think about. I grew up in a family where the cousins were always around, the aunts and uncles were always around, and without knowing it I accumulated this information base of how my relatives behaved in certain situations. As parents, if you have a child that's born to you, you expect that child will fit into that set of norms and that set of family behaviors. In my family it's very common for kids to be really anxious, so if I had an anxious kid it wouldn't surprise me at all."

"To make it physical," Gwen says, "take glasses. If everyone in your family had glasses, you would be watching to see if their eyes got bad so they had to wear glasses. But when you adopt a child, anything is possible. And so you're so afraid you're going to miss something."

"I would imagine," David says, "that you probably thought that Gwen and I were a little bit hypersensitive about Jasper when we brought him to you."

"Actually," I say, "you didn't tell me about your reaction to our first conference until much later, so I didn't know how concerned you were about my reaction to him."

"But as a teacher, you see a child," David continues, "and maybe he seems like he's a little bit slow in some area but he's doing OK and from your point of view there's really no reason for these parents to be so up in arms."

"They're taking him for testing and testing and testing," Gwen says. "If I were looking from the outside, I'd be saying, 'What is with these crazy parents? This poor kid's being put through the mill.' But it's that fear that I'm going to miss something because I don't know what it is that he's bringing into our world."

"I think the other reason that adoptive parents are nervous is that most of us have had to deal with a whole lot of internally generated and externally generated stigmas about 'bringing a stranger into the family,'" David says. "In Gwen's and my experience, when we made the decision to adopt we went out to dinner with her parents, and we were talking about putting together our adoption papers and making a decision about what kind of child we wanted to adopt."

"This was the first time they had heard we were going to adopt," Gwen says.

"We were answering questions. Did we want to adopt an infant?" David continues. "Did we want an older child? Did we want to adopt domestically, or were we going to adopt internationally?

You have to start thinking about things that you didn't have to think about before. You're making racial judgments—am I comfortable having a child that's a different race than mine? Am I comfortable having a child that may have been born with less than optimal pre-natal care? Am I comfortable adopting an older child that may have some significant medical issues? Will I adopt a child who I know has a hole in his heart and is possibly going to need multiple surgeries and go through a lot of problems? These are all choices that an adoptive parent is faced with. Biological parents are only faced with them at the time that they conceive or give birth. And you get what you get. But there's this illusion that you have a choice when you're an adoptive parent.

"So we went out to dinner with Gwen's parents, and we were trying to articulate how we were having these choices that we're supposed to face, and Gwen's father was like, 'I don't know why it's a choice; you just take only the perfect kids. They're not going to palm off defective kids on you. You can't let them do that to you.' And my response was 'This is a person; this is not a toaster. I am not buying an appliance; I am looking at a person. And it's not like this choice is real—it's totally illusory. You can adopt a brand-new baby and it can look perfectly healthy, and then three months down to road it turns out that it's got diabetes or epilepsy.'"

"And you don't bring it back," Gwen says. "Although weirdly enough, when you adopt you can bring it back. For six months, it's not even yours. So you can bring it back. It's called a 'disrupted adoption.' It happens a lot with domestic adoptions that go through the Department of Social Services. With international adoptions it's harder because then you have to actually put them in the DSS system."

"And there's this perception among your family members and your peer group that your adopted child was a choice you made," David says. "So if you got a child that has social issues, medical is-sues, anything else, you made that choice. It's your fault. Whereas if you're a biological parent, you just got stuck with it and you get sympathy."

"Did you expect the adoption to be an issue with your parents?"

"No," Gwen says. "It blew me away totally. That's what was such a horrible thing. My dad just talks before he thinks and I know he didn't mean it. That comment hit me the wrong way, and David got upset and it became a big to-do. And we said something about 'Well, we couldn't care less about race.' And my dad said, 'Well, you don't want to adopt a black baby.' And we said, 'Why? It is not an issue for us.' And he said, 'Then you have too many culture issues.' I burst into tears and we walked out of the restaurant, and we were in the car going home and I was saying, 'I'm disowning my family; I hate these people. I don't know where they came from.' It was horrible. It took about three or four weeks for us to understand where he was coming from and that it wasn't a racial comment so much as it was 'You're taking on a burden; no matter what you do when you adopt, you're taking on a burden. Are you sure you're ready to take that on?' And I'm turning around and saying we don't have a choice.

"Plus when we're adoptive parents we have to pass a test in order to be judged fit to do this. We have to go through a home study, we have to fill out eight million forms, we have to have a medical checkup; you go through so many hurdles for the state or the government to check off, or multiple governments, to say, 'Yes, you're qualified to be a parent.' They stamp you and say, 'You're a good parent,' and then they hand you a child and then you just freeze and say, 'Oh my god, everybody thinks I know what I'm doing.' And we don't know any better than anybody else.

"We adopted Jasper at the same time there was a baby boom in David's extended family. All his cousins were having babies, and they all looked exactly the same. So they were bringing these little blond-haired, blue-eyed babies, and here I show up with my dark-skinned, dark-haired baby that's adopted, and the only experience they had in their family with adoption was negative, and I was very nervous. Everybody said the right thing, but even at that, I was always second-guessing what they were really thinking."

"So your being worried about how they would respond might have affected the way you presented your baby to the family," I say. "Because normally, unless you had a crying, screaming baby, you would expect everyone to love and admire a new baby in the family."

"Exactly. And the screaming, crying baby—that was Kalli. She came into my life, this screaming, crying, projectile-vomiting baby, and I walked in and said, 'Look what I adopted!' And I mean at that point I was waiting for people to say, 'Well, if you're that crazy, go suffer!' I called my mother, crying, and said, 'Mom, I don't even like this baby; how am I supposed to learn to love her?' We never had a babysitter because I was convinced that she was so horrible that if we had someone babysit for her they'd kill her."

"Did you consider taking her back?" I ask. "The six-month rule?"

"No, we never thought of it. No, we knew she was ours. But we knew going in that her birth mother used a lot of drugs; we knew that during her pregnancy."

"We had already faced this question," David says. "We were going to be adopting a drug-addicted and possibly malformed baby with all kinds of social-emotional issues."

"Her birth mother called us at five months," Gwen says, "and said, 'I'm on a heroin binge. I'll be very honest with you. If you don't want this baby I understand. But I'm not stopping.' And so we got off the phone and we said, 'Well what do you do with this?' And I was very frightened and didn't know what to do. David immediately said, 'If not us, who, Gwen?' And he was right there. My approach, typical me, was to get on the computer and look up every conceivable thing that could happen with every conceivable drug. And it made me feel really good. Because there's a lot of hype about what drugs do to babies prenatally—it doesn't really do that much."

"Low birth weight—that's about it." David says.

"And heroin, that's one of the better ones to take. I read all these articles and I came back with 'Isn't this cool!' We knew when our child's birthmother had taken each of the drugs. She was very open and honest with us about that. And when we looked up the effects of each drug during different prenatal exposure periods, we realized we were very lucky. There was really very little for us to worry about."

"Ecstasy was the one we were worried about most," David says, "because there is a certain point during the pregnancy that if you take ecstasy it will cause limb deformities or finger deformities."

"Could you tell her not to take it?" I ask.

"No," Gwen says. "She was taking ecstasy. We couldn't have influenced her to save anything. She wanted to abort this baby, but she was not permitted to because she had had an abortion just a month prior to getting pregnant. They wouldn't let her, medically, get another abortion. So it was kind of tough, but we knew what we were getting into. Well, not really. It's one thing to know what you're getting and it's another to live it."

"There are so many different adoption scenarios," David says, "between domestic closed, domestic open, international, and every single culture in international adoptions; they are all very, very different processes. Every single adoption experience is painful, but it's very, very different in how it's painful."

"Here's another thing," Robert says. "Caleb and Jasper and Katya have all bonded with their parents pretty darn well, but sometimes bonding doesn't happen, and the parents that are having difficulty bonding with their adoptive child are under unbelievable stress. They're wondering, 'Is it me? Is it my child? Is it both of us? What have I done wrong?' They're comparing themselves to other parents. So that's something that's probably important for other adults in their community to be very aware of. The other thing on bonding is that when we brought Katya home I was very uncertain how the extended family was going to bond with her. It turns out it's been fantastic. But I was wondering. I didn't know how Katya's one grandparent was going to bond with her. I didn't know how all the zillion cousins were going to bond with her, or the aunts and uncles. But it's all gone well."

"What led you to worry about that when you might not have given it a thought if she was a natural birth?" I ask.

"It's because there was no experience in my family with adoption. We're the pioneers in the family. I said, 'How is our life going to be different if somebody in our extended family that we're close to is not accepting of either our decision or our child?'

"Last week," Robert says, "at story time before bed, as I do so often, I said, 'Katya, why do I love you so much?' And this last time she says, 'Because you're my daddy.' So that was like complete acceptance. It wasn't 'Because you're my adoptive dad.' Or it wasn't 'Because you came all the way to Russia and got me.' It's just Dad. The relationship is just what it is."

"I had the exact same conversation with Jasper last night," David says. "It was bedtime; I was saying good-night, and I said, 'Do you know why I love you so much?' and he said, 'Because you're my dad.' It's the way it is."

4. The Bar Mitzvah

I find a letter from Caleb in my school mailbox. I get one every now and then, in the shaky handwriting of a beginning writer, a few words—"I miss you" or "How are you?" But this one is different, with my address in perfect script on an envelope with a gold stripe.

I haven't seen him since he came to visit the school a couple of years ago, long-legged, nervous, like an adolescent deer. And now, in my mailbox, is an invitation to his Bar Mitzvah.

I have to admit to some skepticism about the Bar Mitzvah thing. To me, being Jewish wasn't a choice; for better and for worse, it was what I was born to. I had never understood why Golda, an Italian Catholic, had wanted to convert.

Opening the invitation, I think of Caleb helping Jasper climb onto his motorcycle, picture him putting his arm around Ariel when she was crying, and I know I will go. When the day arrives, even though it is pounding rain, an hour's drive on a much-needed Saturday morning, I set out for the temple, expecting to stay the minimum amount of time in order to have him see that I was there for him.

With bad weather and a mistake in driving directions, I am late, walking in just as Caleb is haltingly reading the Sabbath prayers, struggling word by word to say them right. He seems to have special trouble with directions like "turn to page 176," and the rabbi leans over gently to help him. If my grandfather had been there, he would have been saying the prayers at what he considered the proper speed, loudly, the way he did when I was finally allowed to read the four questions in Hebrew at the Passover meal, only because there were no boys left to do the job right. But no one in this audience seems impatient. Caleb proudly walks to the Ark to pick up the Torah, the first five books of the Bible. First Golda and then Katya, Robert, and Lynn are called up to stand with him. They form a procession, walking slowly around the room. Women reach out to touch the Torah with their prayer books, then put the books to their lips; men do the same with their prayer shawls as Caleb comes near. Then he slowly reads the weekly Torah portion in Hebrew, gives his summary and commentary in English, and announces that now he is a man.

The rabbi puts both his hands on Caleb's shoulders, looks in his eyes, and tells us how much Caleb wanted to learn, how he'd always sat in the front row of the class, how he'd asked more questions than any of the other students. The rabbi reminds us that Caleb's Hebrew name is David, after his mother's father; in the Jewish tradition, a child is named after a relative who has died. Caleb, he says, reminds him of King David in two ways—his love of music and his care for his community. For his service project, Caleb has done far more than the required number of hours visiting the elderly at a nursing home specializing in Alzheimer's patients.

I cry—for how hard Caleb must have worked to be able to read the prayer book, for how much I'd wanted to help him get ready for first grade and thought I'd failed, for the friends who still care about him, for Golda, who had the foresight to know that she, a single mother, needed to provide Caleb with traditions, roots, and a community that cares about him, for my misjudging of her and underestimating of him, and because I hadn't failed after all.

Then I drive home in the rain, happy to be wrong.

Recommended Reading

This bibliography is a description of books and articles that have been useful to me, as I have learned about issues affecting adopted children in school. It is not intended to be all-inclusive; rather, it is a list of books that have influenced my own understanding and my work with children from international adoptions.

Talking with Children about Adoption

At home and in the classroom, I have learned that it is important that conversation about adoption take place so frequently that it can be a comfortable subject for discussion, not something reserved only for a special occasion. There are several resources to help this conversation get started.

Picture Books for the Family and for the Classroom

When I look for picture books that will open up issues of adoption in the classroom, I want, first of all, a good story line. I look for characters who were adopted and a narrative that the children love so much they cheer when I begin to read it a second time. Even if the word *adoption* is not mentioned, reading such a book tells the children that adoption is OK; it's something we can think and talk about; it's both normal and interesting.

Kasza, Keiko. *A Mother for Choco.* New York: Putnam Juvenile, 1996. Choco, a small yellow bird with a big blue bill, is looking for his mother. He tries several animal mothers (a giraffe, a penguin, a walrus), but they all say they couldn't be his mother because they don't look like him. Finally he finds Mrs. Bear, whose family is made up of all kinds of different animals that she loves and cares for. You don't have to be adopted to love the fun pictures and the surprise ending, and the message comes through clearly that a mother doesn't have to look the same as her child in order to provide love and care. Recommended for preschool and kindergarten.

Parnell, Peter, and Justin Richardson. *And Tango Makes Three*. New York: Simon and Schuster, 2005. Based on a true story, this book describes a pair of male penguins at the Central Park Zoo who try to make a nest like the other penguin pairs. The zookeeper helps them to hatch an egg and raise a baby penguin. Children love the pictures and the surprise of the story, which encourages discussion of adoption as well as of families with two dads. Recommended for preschool through grade 3.

Rotner, Shelley, and Sheila M. Kelly. *Shades of People*. New York: Holiday House, 2009. This book, with its close-up photographs of children from around the world, will fascinate young children and tell an important story with few words. I love the opening sentences: "Have you noticed that people come in many different shades?" "Not colors, exactly, but shades." Although this is not specifically about adoption, it is a good introduction to racial and ethnic diversity.

Sansone, Adele Sansone. *The Little Green Goose*. New York: North-South Books, 1999. Mr. Goose longs for a chick of his own, "a downy little goose that would call him daddy." Mr. Goose lovingly builds a nest for an egg that needs care, hatching a scaly-skinned, spiky-tailed "green goose" which is clearly a little dinosaur. The "green goose" searches for a mother who looks like him but comes to realize that he truly belongs with Mr. Goose, who gives him unconditional love. The story and illustrations are humorous, and the message of the book is that families can come in many varieties.

Books to Help Adults Talk with Children about Adoption

I first realized that I needed to become more comfortable talking with children about adoption when a child in my class asked me if Jasper had a mom before he was adopted. These are two books that can help children, parents, and teachers answer this and other difficult questions that can arise.

Schoettle, Marilyn. *W.I.S.E. Up Powerbook*. Burtonsville, MD: Center for Adoption Support and Education, 2000. If the structure of a workbook with specific questions to talk about with your child makes it easier to start a discussion, this might be a good choice for you to help a child answer questions about adoption that might come up at school. For ages 6–12.

Stein, Sara Bonnett. *The Adopted One: An Open Family Book for Parents and Children Together*. New York: Walker, 1983. For a more open-ended approach, *The Adopted One* is a wonderful book for children beginning to discuss some of the difficult feelings that can arise around loss and abandonment. Each page includes a story to read to a child and commentary to help adults understand the deeper issues. The children's story is appropriate for children of preschool and kindergarten age, but the adult commentary may also be useful to help older children deal with complex feelings about being adopted.

Books for Parents and Teachers about Issues in Adoption

Of the many books available about adoption, these were particularly useful to me.

McCreight, Brenda. *Parenting Your Adopted Older Child*. Oakland, CA: New Harbinger, 2002. This book gives clear, detailed descriptions of issues that can come up in adopting a child over two years of age, as well as specific suggestions on how to deal with such issues. McCreight is a family and child therapist who specializes in adoption issues, and she has twelve adopted children of her own. It's clear she has tried out these suggestions and found they worked for her—the explanations about attachment problems, learning difficulties, and cross-cultural and transracial adoptions are logical, and her solutions make sense. She also has a website with valuable information about working with children who have attachment issues: http://www.theadoptioncounselor.com/.

Miller, Laurie C. *The Handbook of International Adoption Medicine: A Guide for Physicians, Parents, and Providers*. New York: Oxford University Press, 2005. This book provides invaluable and detailed information from a pediatrician who specializes in adoption medicine. If parents adopting internationally are not able to consult with a pediatrician with this specialty, this book is essential. It contains information about the wide range of problems that can affect internationally adopted children as well as about problems specific to children from a specific country. Dr. Miller explains what parents should know before the adoption, about prenatal exposure to alcohol and drugs, about the transition to the adoptive family, and about infectious disease.

Adoption and School

Is it important for parents and teachers to talk together about a child's adoption? What is the best way to ask a teacher to adapt curriculum that makes an adopted child feel uncomfortable? These and other questions are discussed in these resources:

Evan B. Donaldson Adoption Institute. "Adoption in the Schools: A Lot to Learn; Promoting Equality and Fairness for All Children and Their Families." Evan B. Donaldson Adoption Institute/Center for Adoption Support

and Education, 2006. Available from http://www.adoptioninstitute
.org/publications/. This report is a good place to start looking for ma-
terial on adopted and foster children in school. It explains some of the
reasons that teachers need to learn more about issues of adoption and
foster care; it proposes steps that should be taken to help teachers become
more sensitive to the needs of these children; and it contains an extensive
bibliography.

Wood, Lansing, and Nancy Ng. *Adoption and the Schools: Resources for Parents
and Teachers.* Palo Alto, CA: FAIR (Families Adopting in Response), 2001.
This book is a collection of short pieces about issues that affect adopted
children in school, from how to decide what to tell teachers about a
child's adoption to how to adapt assignments that would otherwise make
adopted children uncomfortable.

Building Community in the Classroom

How can a teacher of young children build a community that supports every
child and encourages an appreciation of differences?

Ashton-Warner, Sylvia. *Teacher.* New York: Simon and Schuster, 1963. This
book showed me (and a whole generation of teachers) that good teaching
begins with understanding what is most important to the children and
builds a curriculum around those passions. Ashton-Warner's concept of
"key vocabulary," teaching reading and writing by using the words that are
most important to each child, was a revolutionary approach in education
and still influences my teaching every day.

Paley, Vivian Gussin. *The Boy on the Beach: Building Community through Play.*
Chicago: University of Chicago Press, 2010.

———. *The Boy Who Would Be a Helicopter: The Uses of Storytelling in the Classroom.* Cambridge, MA: Harvard University Press, 1990.

———. *Wally's Stories.* Cambridge, MA: Harvard University Press, 1981.

———. *You Can't Say You Can't Play.* Cambridge, MA: Harvard University
Press, 1993.

Vivian Paley's work has profoundly influenced my own teaching and
writing. Acting out the children's stories is a key aspect of her work. Such
sharing of one's personal fantasies with friends in a larger group allows a
strong and inclusive community to develop and enables every child to feel
appreciated and cared for. Children love this activity and are motivated to
explain their ideas clearly so they can be acted out as they imagined them.
The development of language skills needed to tell a story clearly and the
feedback the author receives when more information is needed help all

children but are particularly valuable for children who need more experience with expressive and receptive language.

Most of all, I value Paley's unwavering appreciation of children as individuals, her clarity regarding the critical importance of listening carefully to children's play and stories, her delight in finding connections between children and in asking questions that help her to understand them better, her assumption that each child is doing his or her very best to make friends and keep loneliness at bay. "Whenever I think about the children's differences," she writes, (*The Boy Who Would Be a Helicopter*, 47), "my sense of the excitement of teaching mounts."

Understanding Child Development

Children who spent much of their early life without a consistent caregiver may have missed out on important stages of child development, including learning to trust adults and learning to communicate with language. These children may need to go through developmental steps differently from children who have grown up feeling loved and have had a rich early language experience. Understanding child development can help parents and teachers make sense of the many different paths children take through the early years.

Erikson, Erik H. *Childhood and Society.* New York: W. W. Norton, 1950. Erikson's delineation of stages of development, beginning with "Trust vs. Mistrust," helps us understand why a child needs to be cuddled, played with, and talked to in order to develop a sense of the world as a safe place. The way a child learns to balance this tension between trust and mistrust will affect how he or she deals with the tensions of the following stage, "Autonomy vs. Doubt." At each stage, however, there are opportunities to undo damages experienced in the preceding stages. Looking at child development from this constructive point of view helped me to see the importance of laying groundwork for these early stages even as children grow older.

Further, Erikson showed how a child's development is closely connected with the social, historical, and political context in which he or she grows. Understanding connections between culture and development raises valuable questions regarding children from international adoption. What is the relationship between Caleb's Roma roots and his love of drumming? Is Jasper's Cambodian heritage reflected in the satisfaction he finds in careful printing of names and lists, and should I therefore see it as a strength rather than a sign of anxiety? Such questions do not have clear answers but must not be ignored.